YORK NOTES

TESS OF THE D'URBERVILLES

THOMAS HARDY

Notes by Karen Sayer
Revised by Beth Palmer

PEARSON

YORK PRESS

The right of Karen Sayer to be identified as Author
of this Work has been asserted by her in accordance with the
Copyright, Designs and Patents Act 1988

YORK PRESS
322 Old Brompton Road, London SW5 9JH

PEARSON EDUCATION LIMITED
Edinburgh Gate, Harlow,
Essex CM20 2JE, United Kingdom
Associated companies, branches and representatives throughout the world

First published 1998
This new and fully revised edition first published 2005

10 9 8 7 6 5 4 3

ISBN 978–1–2921–3817–6

Illustration on page 68 by Alan Batley
Typeset by Border Consultants
Printed in Slovakia

Photo credits:
Tristan3D/Shutterstock for page 6 / John Gomez/Shutterstock for page 7/ smereka/Shutterstock for page 8 / Andrew
Roland/Shutterstock for page 9 / Nastco/Thinkstock for page 10 / Khomenko Maryna/Shutterstock for page 11 / Chepko Danil
Vitalevich/Shutterstock for page 12 / © Ben Pipe / Alamy Stock Photo/Alamy for page 13 / Makarova Viktoria/Shutterstock for
page 14 / Gyvafoto/Shutterstock for page 15 / bazilfoto/Thinkstock for page 16 / TrotzOlga/Shutterstock for page 17 /
denphumi/Thinkstock for page 18 / Brand X Pictures/Thinkstock for page 19 / phodo/Shutterstock for page 20 / Jessica
Berkowitz/Shutterstock for page 21 / Pixeljoy/Shutterstock for page 22 / Carmen Rieb/Shutterstock for page 23 /
taviphoto/Shutterstock for page 24 / Procy/Shutterstock for page 25 / Gaeme Dawes/Shutterstock for page 26 /
Hieronymus/Shutterstock for page 27 / LiliGraphie/Thinkstock for page 28 / Kovaleva_Ka/Shutterstock for page 29 / Sue
Chillingworth/Shutterstock for page 30 / Filipe Frazao/Shutterstock for page 31 / Marcin Perkowski/Shutterstock for page 32 /
Martin Haas/Shutterstock for page 34 / Paul Wishart/Shutterstock for page 35 / Vitalii Hulai/Shutterstock for page 36 /
yurazaga/Shutterstock for page 37 / ronstik/Shutterstock for page 38 / Oleksandr Kostiuchenko/Shutterstock for page 40 /
Remi Cauzid/Shutterstock for page 41 / BasPhoto/Shutterstock for page 42 / © Loop images Ltd/Alamy for page 44 / Oleksandr
Kavun/Shutterstock for page 46 top / visuall2/Shutterstock for page 46 bottom / kamui29/Shutterstock for page 47 / Martin
Haas/Shutterstock for page 48 / © Buzzshotz/Alamy for page 49 / Zerbor/Shutterstock for page 50 / © North Wind Picture
Archives/Alamy for page 51 / KonstantinChristian/Shutterstock for page 52 / Inga_Ivanova/Shutterstock for page 53 / Africa
Studio/Shutterstock for page 54 / Dmitry Kalinovsky/Shutterstock for page 55 / November Oscar Kilo/Shutterstock for page 57
/ sergign/Shutterstock for page 58 top / asharkyu/Shutterstock for page 58 bottom / Katoosha/Shutterstock for page 59 /
czoborraul/Shutterstock for page 60 top / © Archive pics/Alamy for page 60 bottom / geogphotos/ Alamy for page 61 / Kira
Garmashova/Shutterstock for page 62 / Richard Griffin/Shutterstock for page 63 / Alan Tunnicliffe/Shutterstock for page 65 /
Daniel J. Rao/Shutterstock for page 66 / Savo Ilic/Shutterstock for page 67 / Alexandra Giese/Shutterstock for page 68 /
Alexandr Junek Imaging s.r.o/Shutterstock for page 69 / © iStock/Pencefn for page 70 / Alastair Wallace/Shutterstock for page
71 / Everett-Art/Shutterstock for page 72

CONTENTS

PART ONE: INTRODUCING *TESS OF THE D'URBERVILLES*

How to study and revise *Tess of the D'Urbervilles* 5
Tess of the D'Urbervilles: A snapshot 6

PART TWO: STUDYING *TESS OF THE D'URBERVILLES*

Synopsis 8
Phase the First, Chapters 1–11 10
    Extract analysis: Chapter 4, pages 32–3 13
Phase the Second, Chapters 12–15 18
Phase the Third, Chapters 16–24 20
Phase the Fourth, Chapters 25–34 24
    Extract analysis: Chapter 30, pages 186–8 26
Phase the Fifth, Chapters 35–44 30
Phase the Sixth, Chapters 45–52 34
Phase the Seventh, Chapters 53–9 39
    Extract analysis: Chapter 59, pages 396–8 42
Progress check 43

PART THREE: CHARACTERS AND THEMES

Characters 45
    Tess 46
    Alec 48
    Angel 49
    Other characters 50
Themes
    Loss, inevitability and the passage of time 52
    The natural and conventional 53
    Love 54
    Religion and justice 55
Progress check 56

PART FOUR: GENRE, STRUCTURE AND LANGUAGE

Genre 57
Structure 58
Language 60
Progress check 64

PART FIVE: CONTEXTS AND INTERPRETATIONS

Contexts 65
    Historical context 65
    Settings 66
    Literary context 67
    Comparative texts 67
Critical interpretations 69
Progress check 73

PART SIX: PROGRESS BOOSTER

Assessment focus..74
How to write high-quality responses..................................76
Questions with statements, quotations or viewpoints 78
Comparing *Tess of the D'Urbervilles* with other texts...............80
Using critical interpretations and perspectives 82
Annotated sample answers...84
    Mid-level answer...84
    Good-level answer...86
    Very high-level answer..88
Practice task 90

PART SEVEN: FURTHER STUDY AND ANSWERS

Further reading...91
Literary terms 92
Revision task answers...93
Progress check answers...94
Mark scheme..103

HOW TO STUDY AND REVISE *TESS OF THE D'URBERVILLES*

These Notes can be used in a range of ways to help you read, study and revise for your exam or assessment.

Become an informed and independent reader

Throughout the Notes, you will find the following key features to aid your study:

- **Key context** margin features: these widen your knowledge of the setting, whether historical, social or political. This is highlighted by the AO3 (Assessment Objective 3) symbol to remind you of its connection to aspects you may want to refer to in your exam responses.

- **Key interpretation** boxes (a key part of AO5 on AQA – AO5 is not assessed by Edexcel in relation to *Tess*): do you agree with the perspective or idea that is explained here? Does it help you form your own view on events or characters? Developing your own interpretations is a key element of higher-level achievement at A Level, so make use of this and similar features.

- **Key connection** features (linked to AO4): whether or not you refer to such connections in your exam writing, having a wider understanding of how the novel, or aspects of it, links to other texts or ideas can give you new perspectives on the text.

- **Study focus** panels: these help to secure your own understanding of key elements of the text. Being able to write in depth on a particular point or explain a specific feature will help your writing have a professional and informed tone.

- **Key quotation** features: these identify the effect of specific language choices – you could use these for revision purposes at a later date.

- **Progress booster** features: these offer specific advice about how to tackle a particular aspect of your study, or an idea you might want to consider discussing in your exam responses.

- **Extract analysis** sections: these are vital for you to use either during your reading or when you come back to the text afterwards. These sections take a core extract from a chapter and explore it in real depth, explaining its significance and impact, raising questions and offering interpretations.

Stay on track with your study and revision

Your first port of call will always be your teacher, and you should already have a good sense of how well you are doing, but the Notes offer you several ways of measuring your progress.

- **Revision task**: throughout the Notes, there are some challenging, but achievable, written tasks for you to do relevant to the section just covered. Suggested answers are supplied in **Part Seven**.

- **Progress check**: this feature comes at the end of **Parts Two** to **Five**, and contains a range of short and longer tasks which address key aspects of the Part of the Notes you have just read. Below this is a grid of key skills which you can complete to track your progress, and rate your understanding.

- **Practice task** and **Mark scheme**: use these features to make a judgement on how well you know the text and how well you can apply the skills you have learned.

Most importantly, enjoy using these Notes and see your knowledge and skills improve.

The edition used in these Notes is the Penguin Classics edition, 2003.

A02 PROGRESS BOOSTER

You can choose to use the Notes as you wish, but as you read the novel it can be useful to read over the **Part Two** summaries and analysis in order to embed key events, ideas and developments in the **narrative**.

A02 PROGRESS BOOSTER

Don't forget to make full use of **Parts Three** to **Five** of the Notes during your reading of the novel. You may have essays to complete on genre, or key themes, or on the impact of specific settings, and can therefore make use of these in-depth sections. Or you may simply want to check out a particular idea or area as you're reading or studying the novel in class.

A01 PROGRESS BOOSTER

Part Six: Progress booster will introduce you to different styles of question and how to tackle them; help you to improve your expression so that it has a suitably academic and professional tone; assist you with planning and use of evidence to support ideas; and, most importantly, show you three sample exam responses at different levels with helpful AO-related annotations and follow-up comments. Dedicating time to working through this Part will be something you won't regret.

TESS OF THE D'URBERVILLES: A SNAPSHOT

A controversial novel

Thomas Hardy's *Tess*, first published as a novel in 1891, continues to inspire admiration and debate. Many critics have treated Tess like a real person and asked, as the Duchess of Abercorn did at the time of publication, 'Do you support her or not?' The debate over whether Tess was raped or seduced, whether she is a total or partial victim, a justified or blameworthy murderer still rages. But Tess is a complex character who cannot be pinned down. She is both a victim and a murderer and this is what makes *Tess of the D'Urbervilles* so bewitching.

It is also easy to become fascinated by the extraordinary texture of Hardy's writing. Hardy uses idiosyncratic language to create a feeling of involvement which, in turn, helps us to see the individual and even the mundane from a new perspective.

Hardy's revisions

When Hardy first attempted to get his novel serialised, he was rejected by several magazines due to its treatment of seduction and illegitimate birth. He soon realised that he would need to edit his work and removed all references to Tess's seduction and to her child, while Angel Clare had to carry the milkmaids across the flood by wheelbarrow, rather than in his arms. *Tess* finally came out as a weekly serial in the *Graphic* from 4 July to 26 December 1891 – it was published simultaneously in *Harper's Bazaar* in the United States.

The edited, serialised version was published as a book after serialisation, but it took some time and several editions before the text finally came together in its complete form. This was because Hardy continued to work steadily on the novel, writing and rewriting it. The first, serialised edition therefore came out in 1891, but *Tess* was not really stable as a text until the 1912 'definitive' Macmillan *Wessex Novels* edition was published. It is this later edition that is now usually reprinted as the final text, though Hardy continued to make minor changes after this date.

Gender politics

The 1890s was a period in which gender inequality was part of everyday life. Women would not be expected to undertake the same work as men, or get paid the same wages for their work. After decades of protest a few women from privileged backgrounds were starting to gain some access to higher education and professional roles but such opportunities would have been unavailable to a young woman in Tess Durbeyfield's social position.

Such a sexual double standard meant that women were held to a higher standard of sexual morality than men. Sex outside of marriage often led to serious social difficulties for women in the nineteenth century. But marriage itself did not always offer women a safe haven and divorce was very difficult to obtain, particularly for women without money or status. At the time of publication Hardy's novel was morally sensitive. The central character is, of course, described in the subtitle as 'pure', but she has an illegitimate child and becomes involved in an adulterous relationship. Hardy is one of a number of writers who attempted to question the sexual double standard. He insists on Tess's innocence throughout the novel.

KEY INTERPRETATION   **A05**

Serialised publication in magazines expanded rapidly during the nineteenth century and some editors put pressure on authors to conform to certain standards of format, style and content. Several critics have considered how publication in the serial format caused Hardy to censor his first version of *Tess*.

KEY CONNECTION   **A04**

'New Woman' writers of the 1890s, including novelists like Olive Schreiner and Sarah Grand, were seeking to open out the possibilities available to women. They, and their fictional characters, often rejected marriage and motherhood in favour of less conventional lifestyles.

Hardy and rural life

Thomas Hardy (1840–1928) was born near Dorchester and many of his novels, including *Tess*, are set in his native county of Dorset. Villages and towns are recognisable but are given fictionalised names.

Hardy is sometimes mistakenly described as a self-taught peasant. In fact he had an excellent formal education and had already become a successful architect before he entered the literary circles of his day. Hardy therefore certainly moved up the social ladder during his life, but he never entirely belonged to the labouring class to which his family was only ever tangentially connected. He wrote about labourers as a somewhat distanced observer; we often see Tess as if viewed from above. He did not write for the labouring classes but for the educated metropolitan public, although his writing did often feature rural customs such as the club-walking with which Hardy introduces Tess to his readers.

Study focus: Key issues to explore **A02**

As you study the text and revise for the exam, keep in mind these key elements and ideas:

- The concept of purity and why Tess is described as a 'pure woman'
- The worthiness of Angel as the object of Tess's love
- Inequalities between the lives of men and women
- The relationship between faith and doubt
- The nature of fate
- The relationship between the individual and their environment
- The relationship between past and present
- The hardships of rural life and agricultural work
- The relations between the classes

In each case, make sure you develop your own interpretations and, with the help of these Notes, prepare to argue your viewpoint on them.

SYNOPSIS

Phase the First: The Maiden

The novel, as the title suggests, is about a young woman, whose name is Tess Durbeyfield. It is structured around seven phases which reflect the pattern of her short life. In the first phase, Tess's father finds out about his ancestors – the D'Urbervilles – and gets so drunk in celebration of this, even though 'There are several families among the cottagers ... of almost equal lustre', according to the parson (Chapter 1, p. 9), that he cannot drive to market. Tess goes instead, and the family's horse dies in a terrible accident.

The remorseful Tess, under encouragement from her mother and father, goes to a Mrs D'Urberville to seek help. Mrs D'Urberville, however, is not really, as they all suppose, a distant relative. The surname has simply been assumed by a successful commercial family who have recently moved to the area. While on her errand, Tess meets Mrs D'Urberville's son Alec, who finally arranges for Tess to be employed on his mother's estate. While Tess is there, Alec persistently pursues, and eventually dishonours her.

Phase the Second: Maiden No More

In the second phase, Tess, now pregnant, returns home from Trantridge. Guilt-ridden and ashamed, only venturing out at dusk, Tess hides in her family's cottage. Once she has had her illegitimate child, Sorrow, she goes back to work and finds that she is generally accepted by her community. The child, however, dies and though she hopes to save his soul by carrying out her own baptism, he is still buried in an unmarked grave. Tess stays in the village for a while, but eventually decides that it would be better to start afresh somewhere new.

Phase the Third: The Rally

In the third phase, Tess leaves home again and this time takes work for the spring and summer on a dairy farm far away from everyone she knows. While working at Talbothays she meets Angel Clare, a clergyman's son – he in fact first appears, very briefly, at the beginning of the book. He is working at the dairy in order to learn something about farming. He would have gone to university like his brothers, but for the fact that he has rejected his family's very rigid form of Christianity.

Phase the Fourth: The Consequence

Tess and Angel begin to fall in love and this is very hard for Tess, who cannot quite bring herself to tell Angel about Alec and Sorrow, though she knows that she should do so. The tension builds as Tess and Angel move towards marriage. She tries to write a letter to him, in which she confesses everything, but he never receives it and the fourth phase ends on their wedding night, as Angel confesses his own youthful misdemeanours.

Phase the Fifth: The Woman Pays

As we enter the fifth phase, Tess finally confesses everything. Unable to see the parallels between their previous experiences, Angel shuns her and declares that she is no longer the woman he loved: 'You were one person; now you are another' (Chapter 35, p. 228). Tess goes home and Angel emigrates to Brazil. He has left her money to take care of herself, but after helping her parents repair their house – they are deceived by Tess into believing in a reconciliation, and therefore have high expectations of her new-found wealth – she is left with very little to live on and must find a job for the winter. She starts working at Flintcomb-Ash, where the work is particularly hard. Her old friends from the dairy farm are there and they eventually persuade her to seek help from Angel's family – the Clare family are also oblivious to the failure of the marriage. However, she overhears Angel's brothers talking disparagingly about the marriage, so she moves on quickly without seeking his parents' aid. While walking back, she is surprised to see Alec, recently converted to Christianity, preaching in a barn.

Phase the Sixth: The Convert

In the sixth phase, Alec's faith is tried by Tess. He becomes newly fascinated by her and offers to marry her, but when she tells him that she cannot, he persists in pursuing her. Alec loses his faith, but still offers to help her and her family. For a while Tess manages to fend him off, but when she suddenly has to return home to look after her mother and her father, she begins to weaken. Soon after this, Tess's father dies and her family are forced to leave their cottage. Again, Alec appears and offers help, and, as the family's new arrangements fall through, her determination to have nothing more to do with him begins to crumble.

Phase the Seventh: Fulfilment

In the seventh and final phase, Angel returns from Brazil. Thanks to his experiences abroad, he has changed. He eventually tracks Tess and Alec down to a lodging house in Sandbourne. He seeks reconciliation but, seeing that she is well provided for, quickly leaves. Tess goes back to her rooms in distress and, furious that Alec had lied to her about Angel ever coming back to her, she murders him. She runs after Angel. They manage to outwit their pursuers and are blissfully happy for a week. They are finally tracked down at Stonehenge where Tess makes Angel promise that he will care for her younger sister 'Liza-Lu. Tess is arrested and, in the final chapter, hanged, watched from afar by 'two speechless gazers bent themselves down to the earth, as if in prayer' (Chapter 59, p. 398).

A01 PROGRESS BOOSTER

Hardy's novel is long and its plot involves several different settings and journeys. It also involves several interlocking groups of characters. You will need to consider how Tess interacts with each of these groups, and whether these interactions change Tess's character as the story progresses.

KEY CONTEXT   **A03**

The parson tells Jack Durbeyfield that he can trace his lineage back to Sir Pagan D'Urberville. Pagan was a relatively rare Norman-French name, related to Payn, but the word carries a number of useful connotations for Hardy, including reference not only to heathen and non-Christian practices and beliefs, but also, via *paganus* and *pagus*, to rusticity and the countryside. The French *pagus*, in particular, refers to a landmark fixed in the earth.

KEY CONTEXT   **A03**

Hardy derived the fictional name D'Urberville from the real name Turberville. The Turbervilles were lords of the manor during the thirteenth century in Bere Regis, Dorset (Hardy's Kingsbere). Durbeyfield is also close to the related Turberville derivative Turbyfield. The Turberville name also occurs with reference to King William I's creation of what were known as marcher lordships, each of which had almost king-like prerogatives. Among these was the marcher lord Robert FitzHamon, Lord of Glamorgan, whose retinue included one Sir Payn de Turberville (nicknamed 'the Demon'). Though not given land by FitzHamon, de Turberville nonetheless acquired it by taking over the lordship of Coity Castle, Wales.

PHASE THE FIRST: THE MAIDEN, CHAPTER 1

Summary

- While walking home from market one May evening, Jack Durbeyfield meets Parson Tringham. Jack wants to know why the parson has been calling him 'Sir John' recently.

- The parson tells him that he is descended from 'the ancient and knightly family of the D'Urbervilles' (p. 8), a family that is now 'extinct in the male line' and that he should reflect on 'how are the mighty fallen' (p. 9).

- Jack, who has been drinking, decides to celebrate. He sends a boy for a carriage from The Pure Drop Inn, complete with a noggin of rum on account. He gives the boy a shilling, asks him to tell his wife to stop washing and for them 'at home' (p. 11) to cook him a fine dinner.

- Just as the boy sets out a brass band can be heard in the distance; it is the 'women's club-walking' (p. 11) in which, the boy reminds Jack, his daughter is participating.

Analysis

A real story about real people

Detailed description and dialect generate a feeling that Hardy is telling the reader a real story about real people, engendering a sense of **verisimilitude**. Class and social mobility come to the fore in the relationship between Jack and the parson. There is extensive use of historical and geographical detail – in the first sentence we find reference to 'the adjoining Vale of Blakemore or Blackmoor' (p. 7) – and the peasantry are linked both to the locality and to the broader historical process, the history of England.

A02

Progress booster: Hardy's use of foreshadowing

Look out for links and connections in the novel. This opening chapter introduces the issue of Tess's ancestry and later on Tess will visit the tombs of her forebears, as described to Jack. Many future events are hinted at in the chapter and this extensive use of **foreshadowing** is typical of the earlier phases of the novel. The family's ongoing decline seems inevitable and Tess's fate seems sealed. Here we see that Jack Durbeyfield is already drunk, in addition to which he immediately starts racking up debts and giving away money. Jack is proud like his ancestors, and we will see the same characteristic emerge in Tess.

Make sure you understand how Hardy's use of foreshadowing is key to the theme of the inevitability of loss and suffering and how it builds during the novel.

PHASE THE FIRST, CHAPTERS 2–3

Summary

- The village women, including Tess Durbeyfield, are celebrating the coming of spring. Tess is embarrassed by her father Jack's behaviour.

- The women begin dancing. They are watched by three young gentlemen, one of whom, Angel, decides to join in. Angel does not dance with Tess but then reproaches himself for missing the opportunity.

- Tess returns home. Her mother, Joan, passes on the news of the family's good fortune and also tells Tess that Jack's health is failing. Joan joins Jack in celebrating their good fortune at the local pub, Rolliver's.

- Tess is left to look after her brothers and sisters until, tired of waiting, she sends her little brother Abraham after them. When he fails to return she goes to get them back herself, as her father is due to set out on a delivery in the early hours.

Analysis

Introducing Tess

We meet Tess for the first time in Chapter 2. Again, future events in the novel are **foreshadowed** and description is predominant. Tess, for instance, who is 'a fine and handsome girl … [with a] mobile peony mouth and large innocent eyes … wore a red ribbon in her hair, and was the only one of the white company who could boast of such a pronounced adornment' (p. 14). Here we see Tess as an innocent country maid but the complexities of her character that, in part, give rise to her later misfortunes, begin to show.

Tess seems to be part of the landscape, in contrast to Angel, who moves through it very quickly. Hardy also shows Tess as a divided character from the start. She is educated and yet remains a peasant, she is simultaneously more ambitious and more cautious than her parents, she is linked to both ancient tradition and a pull to modernity. We are told early on that she effectively speaks two languages, dialect at home, and more standard English – which she has learned at the National School – when appropriate. She is aware of the need to present herself differently depending on the situation and the audience.

A03

Study focus: Class as a social marker

Hardy's narratorial emphasis on the importance of the imaginative lives of individuals – regardless of class – is set up in this chapter. All the girls participating in the dance are said to have a 'private little sun for her soul to bask in' (p. 14), although of course it is Tess on whom the narrator focuses. Most of the characters we meet see class as a significant social marker and of the three well-educated brothers watching the dance, two scorn dancing with working-class girls.

The domestic setting of the Durbeyfield family strikes Tess's senses with 'unspeakable dreariness' (p. 20). The narrator evokes the daily grind of household tasks – washing, cooking, tending children – as unending in this family placed near the bottom of the social scale. Notice how both Tess's parents see her as more socially mobile than themselves and therefore key to the family's possibilities of escape from poverty.

A03 KEY CONTEXT

Angel was a name suggested to Hardy by a memorial in Stinsford parish church. The most popular first names in the UK in 1880 were Mary and William.

A03 KEY CONTEXT

Tess has passed the Sixth Standard at the National School. National schools existed throughout the country and were one of the main ways in which the poor could have access to education until the 1870 Education Act, which made education available to all, and the 1891 Education Act, which made education free. Tess has benefited from some schooling but her childhood ambition of becoming a teacher is thwarted by the needs of her family.

It was commonplace in the nineteenth century for antiquarians like Parson Tringham to study aristocratic lineages. It was also commonplace for 'new money' to buy into the status and authority of an aristocratic name. Simon Stoke, the recently deceased father of Alec D'Urberville, made his money as a merchant but on retiring from business and moving to the South of England he chose a 'name not quite so well remembered there' (p. 39).

In his *Essay on the Principle of Population* (1798), Malthus proposed that the population would naturally grow faster than humanity's ability to feed itself, and discussed natural and artificial ways in which population growth might be checked. Many Victorian writers were interested in Malthus's ideas – Charles Dickens, for example, critiqued them in *A Christmas Carol*. Here, Tess 'felt Malthusian vexation with her mother for thoughtlessly giving her so many little sisters and brothers' (p. 37). A woman like Tess would probably not have heard of Malthus but she would have been very familiar with the problems encountered by an increasing family with decreasing resources.

PHASE THE FIRST, CHAPTERS 4–5

Summary

- Joan remembers that there is a rich woman living in Trantridge called D'Urberville. Assuming her to be a relative, she considers sending Tess over 'to claim kin' (p. 27). The speculations as to what may come of claiming kin continue until Tess arrives. Jack has drunk too much and is helped home by his wife and daughter.
- When the time comes for Jack to leave for Casterbridge market, he cannot get up. Tess offers to go if Abraham, her younger brother, will accompany her.
- They drive through the night talking about fate, but they doze off and, as their wagon drifts to the far side of the road, the morning mail-cart ploughs into them. Their horse, Prince, bleeds to death.
- Tess blames herself for the catastrophe and the consequent decline in her family's fortunes, and she agrees to visit Mrs D'Urberville.
- She reaches The Slopes, the home of the D'Urbervilles and is intercepted by Mrs D'Urberville's son, Alec.
- When Tess explains her errand, he calls her 'my pretty girl' (p. 41) and shows her around. The Slopes is a decorative hobby farm, built purely for pleasure, so that 'Everything looked like money – like the last coin issued from the Mint' (p. 38).
- Alec gives Tess some strawberries and makes her eat one from his hand. He gives her roses and gets her to place some in her bosom. He promises that he will try to help.

Analysis

Omniscient narration

Hardy uses an **omniscient narrator** here. This provides us with information that Tess does not have access to, to signal the significant part that Alec will play in her destiny, and to provide us with some of the philosophical framework of the novel. The individual characters are much more partial in their views. Jack and Joan Durbeyfield do not have a good grasp of history, or of the moral dangers they are exposing Tess to – recognised by some of the other drinkers as getting 'green malt in flower' (p. 28) – although they are sensitive to economic need. Tess herself is naive and does not understand the full significance of Alec's advances. But Hardy shows she is sensitive to the fact that the D'Urbervilles may not be all that they seem. She is described as 'hesitating', 'falter[ing]' and 'confounded' (pp. 40–1) in her meeting with Alec, not knowing how to converse with a gentleman who speaks to her so informally.

Omniscient narration also gives Hardy the opportunity to distort time, and we learn more about Tess's character through the short **flashback** to her childhood. Her early friendships and success at school have been displaced by her responsibilities as a quasi-maternal figure for her younger brothers and sisters.

Revision task 1: Moments of foreboding

Make notes on moments in the novel where the narrator seems to look to Tess's future fate, even while discussing the present moment. In particular, focus on:

- The kind of symbolism used in these moments of prescience
- The effect these moments have on the tone of the novel

EXTRACT ANALYSIS: CHAPTER 4, PAGES 32–3

From: 'Left to his reflections' to 'Prince is killed!'

This early passage in *Tess of the D'Urbervilles* is a turning point in the novel. Tess Durbeyfield and her younger brother Abraham have set out late at night to take some beehives to market for their father, Jack, who is too drunk to get up and drive the cart himself. He has been celebrating the discovery that he is a descendant of the ancient and aristocratic D'Urbervilles. As they travel through the night, Tess and Abraham doze off and have a terrible accident; their horse, vital to the family's income, is killed. Later on, because Tess feels responsible for the accident, she seeks help from a Mrs D'Urberville, whom her family wrongly suppose to be a distant relative.

Just before the passage begins, Tess and Abraham have been discussing their fate, the feeling that they have been born in a 'blighted' world, and its largely pessimistic tone is framed by the rhetorical question that Abraham raises just before their horse dies: 'How would it have been if we had pitched on a sound one?' (p. 32). Abraham is a young child but he has already been exposed to many of life's hardships and inequalities and, like Tess, his outlook seems to be a tragic one. The passage also raises the question of the fatalism of the novel, suggesting that the possibilities for happiness might already be foreclosed in this 'blighted' world.

We see the world from Tess's **point of view** as she carefully settles Abraham down to sleep and begins to muse over her father's pride, her mother's ambition. This is why we are as ignorant as she of the accident; we have, in a sense, dozed off with her. Hardy successfully creates a feeling of someone suddenly waking up in confusion by describing what she sees and hears, rather than what has happened. In this way we feel Tess's horror and can better understand why she feels that she has allowed the horse to be killed.

Tess often slips into dream-like states at key moments. In the passage leading up to Prince's death she drifts off and enters a state of awareness in which she seems to be drawn outside herself. While in this state, Tess glimpses the future in which both of her gentlemanly suitors will scorn her 'shrouded knightly ancestry' (p. 32). This is an experience which she describes in Chapter 18 as the soul leaving the body, and is suggested here by the transformation of the landscape, which becomes ever more fantastical. The real and the imagined are interwoven in Tess's dreamscape, such as when 'the occasional heave of the wind became the sigh of some immense sad soul' (p. 32). As with other moments where Tess enters a reverie, it could be argued that Hardy is reinforcing the point that she is not responsible for her tragic fate.

A03 KEY CONTEXT

Prince is an old horse, but an important member of the Durbeyfield family, vital to their livelihood. Farm animals are important in Tess's life and she enjoys working with the chickens at Mrs D'Urberville's and milking the cows at Talbothays. To find out more about animals in nineteenth-century English thought, see Harriet Ritvo, *The Animal Estate: The English and Other Creatures in Victorian England* (Penguin, 1990).

The death of the horse is a financial calamity for the Durbeyfields, as Tess is quick to realise. This simple economic fact will lead her into the clutches of the deathly figure she has dreamed about: Alec D'Urberville. But it is also an omen. The passage is graphic and brutal; we see Tess peacefully falling asleep on the dark road, suddenly awakened by utter disaster for her and her family and powerless to stem the tide of Prince's lifeblood. The passage clearly prefigures that in Chapter 11 when she falls asleep and is penetrated by Alec D'Urberville. She will lose her innocence, stand for as long as she can, then fall, just like Prince.

KEY INTERPRETATION **A05**

For an extended discussion of the meanings attached to the use of the colour red in *Tess*, and especially images of red on white, see Tony Tanner, 'Colour and Movement in Hardy's *Tess of the D'Urbervilles*', in Ian Watt, ed., *The Victorian Novel: Modern Essays in Criticism* (Oxford University Press, 1971).

This effect is made clearer by the play of red on white in which Tess, whiter still than her surroundings, has been tinctured by blood. The language at this point is deliberately scientific, for example the pool of blood is described as 'assuming the iridescence of coagulation' (p. 33) in the dawn light. In **juxtaposition** to the pragmatism of the mail-cart man, and with the waking birds, the prismatic (brilliantly and varyingly coloured) play of sunlight suggests the total indifference of nature to Tess's troubles. The narrative moves from a distanced authorial comment, in which the narrator uses very abstract and Latinate words and phrases, to a more immediate dramatisation of the scene at hand, then back towards a remoter stance again as the scene closes. These shifts in narrative perspective, like the use of scientific language, place Tess's plight in the larger context of an uncaring universe.

Revision task 2: Directing the scene

Consider the issues facing a director adapting a novel like *Tess of the D'Urbervilles* for film. How would you direct this scene? Make notes on:

● The different points of view and how you might render the changes of pace between Tess's dream state and her horrified awakening

● The visual aspects of the scene – what impact would these have on costume and colour?

PHASE THE FIRST, CHAPTERS 6–7

Summary

- Tess travels home, decked out in the flowers Alec picked for her. Of all the omens she encounters that day, the only one she notices is 'a thorn of the rose remaining in her breast [that] accidentally pricked her chin' (p. 44).

- Tess is asked to go and work on the D'Urberville estate, but is reluctant to agree.

- Alec arrives at the Durbeyfield's house. Joan is convinced he will marry Tess.

- Tess sets aside her ambition to be a teacher, to help her family.

- Tess gets ready to leave in her working clothes but her mother washes her hair and asks Tess to change into her best clothes.

- Tess is collected by Alec in his gig. She is reluctant to get in but at last they drive away.

- That night Joan wishes she had made further enquiries about the young man's character; still, she assures herself, 'if he don't marry her afore he will after' (p. 53).

Analysis

Trading possibilities

The desire to help her family prompts Tess to act selflessly, against her better judgement; this thematic pattern will be repeated when Alec tries to persuade Tess to take up with him again after Clare has left her. Tess is expected to trade her womanliness, not just her labour, to help her family. The Durbeyfields are not as naive as they might seem. Jack is well aware of the financial possibilities of trading in names. He says he will sell the name and speculates about the possible price. Joan is more interested in Tess's marketability as an attractive young woman, although she does, at least partially, recognise the dangers her daughter will face.

Study focus: Ideal femininity **A01**

Tess puts herself in her mother's hands when preparing for her departure. She washes and brushes her hair and this, combined with the 'airy fullness' of the white frock, 'imparted to her developing figure an amplitude which belied her age' (p. 49). She is still a naive child in many ways but she looks like a woman. When Tess leaves the cottage she is not herself, but an idealised image of herself, and this is a key theme in the book. Note that many of Tess's troubles arise from the fact that men like Alec misread and idealise her.

Key quotation: A lady? **A01**

On page 52, the youngest Durbeyfield sees Alec persuading Tess to ride in his gig and asks, "Is dat the gentleman-kinsman who'll make Sissy a lady?" We already know that Alec is not a kinsman and we suspect that his intentions towards Tess are not gentlemanly. The young child's question holds **ironic** potential and gives Joan Durbeyfield some misgivings about letting her daughter go.

A03 KEY CONTEXT

In the nineteenth century, working-class women's 'respectability' depended in part on the type of paid employment they took. At this point, working with poultry and young farm animals was seen to be quite appropriate for girls and women.

A05 KEY INTERPRETATION

It was relatively common practice among the rural working class, much to the horror of urban middle-class reformers, to marry only once a baby was on the way, and it is to this that Joan Durbeyfield alludes. To start considering how issues of class might fit into a feminist analysis, you could read John Goode's 'Woman and the Literary Text' in Juliet Mitchell and Ann Oakley, eds., *The Rights and Wrongs of Women* (Penguin, 1976), which analyses the ways in which Tess, like all Victorian women, must trade on her femininity. See also Kristin Brady's chapter on 'Thomas Hardy and Matters of Gender' in *The Cambridge Companion to Thomas Hardy* (2006).

PHASE THE FIRST, CHAPTERS 8–9

Summary

- Alec drives off with Tess, who quickly becomes alarmed at his reckless driving.
- He says that he will drive more carefully if she will let him kiss her cheek. She agrees, but dodges him and, though 'D'Urberville gave her the kiss of mastery' (p. 56), she then wipes the kiss off.
- Before the next downward slope begins she loses her hat and once out of the cart refuses to get back in. They exchange harsh words, but finally Alec's temper cools and they walk on, Tess still on the ground, Alec in the gig.
- Tess starts work at The Slopes. The poultry, which are treated like pets, live in an old cottage and Tess must take them up to her blind mistress for daily inspection.
- Alec teaches Tess how to whistle for the bullfinches in Mrs D'Urberville's bedroom. Slowly, he gets Tess to accept him.

Analysis

Leaving home

As she crosses from the vale to Trantridge, Tess moves **metaphorically** from childhood to womanhood. We have already seen how the narrator has pointed out Tess's seeming maturity in relation to her actual years and in comparison to her parents' childish irresponsibility. This is the point at which Tess also becomes an itinerant character within the novel, always on the move. Such characters are common within Hardy's work, such as Michael Henchard in *The Mayor of Casterbridge* (1886).

Tess's fate in Alec's hands

Alec's intentions are made clear here; we see that he is a manipulator. We also learn that he is reckless, cruel and violent. There are parallels between Alec's mastery of the horse and his determination to master Tess. The reckless speed at which he drives the gig is an attempt to manipulate Tess by putting her in dangerous situations where she has little choice but to accept his will. The cigar that he smokes seems to be a quasi-phallic symbol of his power over Tess. The focus on his teeth and lips (echoing the narrator's earlier emphasis on Tess's own mouth) makes him seem even more like a predator. His language swings from exhortation: "Let me put one little kiss on those holmberry lips" (p. 55), to violent oaths , making his character appear rash and unpredictable.

The caged bird

The issue of class is highlighted by the narrator's comments about the cottage in which the fowl are kept and the fact that Tess becomes 'more pliable under [Alec's] hands than a mere companionship would have made her' (p. 62), because she is dependent upon Mrs D'Urberville and therefore, ultimately, upon Alec himself. The way in which the old inhabitants were removed from this cottage **foreshadows** the way in which Tess's family will be removed from theirs in Chapter 51. Tess is trapped, like a caged bird, as Alec whistles to her. She is metaphorically trapped by her class and her gender, and by her obligations to her family. The chapter ends with suspense, with Tess being stalked by Alec, or perhaps by fate.

KEY CONNECTION

Alec's cruel manipulation of Tess could be likened to the behaviour of another nineteenth-century anti-hero – Heathcliff, from Emily Brontë's *Wuthering Heights* (1847). Although Heathcliff does not come from a privileged economic background like Alec, both characters are obsessive towards their respective heroines. Both also leave the narrative for a large part of the book and return seemingly changed.

KEY CONNECTION

The image of the caged bird, and its association with Woman's position, became almost emblematic in nineteenth-century literature and art. For example, see Elizabeth Barrett Browning's poem *Aurora Leigh* (1857).

PHASE THE FIRST, CHAPTERS 10–11

Summary

- Tess goes to a fair in Chaseborough. She does not want to return alone, so stays very late at a dance. Alec offers her a lift home, but she declines.

- Having had too much to drink, Tess and her friends argue. Tess decides to leave them just as Alec appears – she impulsively jumps up behind him and is whisked away.

- As they slow to a walk the fog thickens, and Alec presses Tess to treat him like a lover.

- Tess realises that they have not been travelling towards Trantridge. Alec is unclear about their location and leaves her with his horse while he finds out where they are.

- On his return he finds her asleep and bends down to feel her breath on his face and the tears on her lashes. Hardy suggests that Alec rapes Tess.

Analysis

Study focus: Myth and dance **A03**

Notice the extensive reference to myth in the dance scene. Dance is often symbolic of the success or failure of a community for Hardy. This shows Hardy is not intending to achieve a completely **naturalist** evocation of English peasant life. As we move from **realist** commentary into an otherworldly description of folk dance, we find that Tess's future is **ironically** prefigured in references to classical figures who have escaped pursuit.

What's missing?

Most of this section was missing from the *Graphic* edition. The sexual implications of the scene meant that it had to be censored, and even now what actually happens between Tess and Alec remains unclear, as Hardy simply tells us that an 'immeasurable chasm was to divide our heroine's personality thereafter from that previous self of hers who stepped from her mother's door to try her fortune at Trantridge poultry-farm' (p. 74). The fog and mist – symbols that are used repeatedly in the novel – work **metaphorically**, like the references to the primeval wood, to suggest sexual impropriety. The references to Tess's ancestors add to this and contribute to the pervasive sense of fatalism. The chapter is tense and drawn out, due to the contrast between Tess and Alec's dialogue, the descriptions of the rising fog, the slow movement of the horse, and the stillness of the final scene.

Progress booster: Reappearances **A02**

We are introduced to two incidental characters here – the Queen of Spades and the Queen of Diamonds – who reappear in Chapter 43. Alec's sudden appearance and 'red coal of a cigar' (p. 64) prefigures his devilish entry in Chapter 50. There are also parallels with Chapter 4; in both cases drunkenness allows the rural working class to feel somewhat more elevated and content than usual. Tess is clearly not like the others, though, as she rises above their earthy pleasures. Make sure you can write about how Hardy uses these structural reappearances in the novel.

A05 KEY INTERPRETATION

For a discussion of the relationship between dance and constructions of community in Hardy's writing, see Simon Gatrell, *Thomas Hardy and the Proper Study of Mankind* (Macmillan, 1993).

PHASE THE SECOND: MAIDEN NO MORE, CHAPTER 12

Summary

- Tess walks home early one morning, four months after her arrival at Trantridge.
- Alec catches her up, berates her for her unannounced departure and offers her a lift. During the conversation that follows, he admits that he has done wrong, is a 'bad fellow' (p. 77) and offers compensation as he has apparently done before.
- Tess refuses his help and goes on alone. She meets a labourer whose painted religious slogans sting her conscience.
- At home, she tells her mother that she should have warned her about men.

Analysis

Alec's offers

KEY CONTEXT **A03**

Hardy lost his own Christian faith at some point in the 1860s, possibly due to his reading of the humanist philosopher Auguste Comte and John Stuart Mill's writing against religion in *On Liberty*. Hardy chooses to show how religious conviction can be damaging – as here, where the interpretation of a biblical slogan seems to make Tess a sinner. But he also highlights the humanity to be found when acting on Christian principles, for example in Angel's father's charitable actions.

The end of this chapter was very different in the *Graphic* edition, with Tess being tricked into a false marriage with Alec. It is worth considering the different moral implications of that association, which allowed Tess to believe they were married, and the rather vaguer relationship that is described in the revised version. In the revised version, Tess's eventual acceptance of Angel's offer seems much more morally defensible. The economics of sexual relationships between the classes are made quite explicit in Alec's attempts to help Tess financially and in her refusal, on the grounds that she would then become his 'creature' (p. 77). This offer is essentially reiterated in Chapter 46 and the overall tenor of the conversation is repeated several times throughout Phase the Sixth, suggesting that Alec is seeking to 'buy' Tess. Here, Tess scorns his offer and wants to leave Alec behind entirely.

Study focus: Biblical signs **A02**

When Tess encounters the sign painter and reads his biblical slogans we are told that 'the words entered Tess with accusatory horror' (p. 80). Again, Tess is penetrated, this time symbolically, and once again the colour red – here, a 'staring vermillion' (pp. 79–80) – is used to highlight moments of strain on Tess's self and psyche. The painter of texts appears again in Chapter 44, while Alec is preaching. The red texts themselves act as **metaphorical** moral boundaries – 'THOU, SHALT, NOT, COMMIT' (p. 80) in particular **foreshadows** Tess's later experiences and difficulties. Notice how the painter's choice and use of texts suggests an inflexible sense of religious morality.

Key quotation: Innocence or ignorance? **A01**

On returning home, Tess asks her mother, "Why didn't you tell me there was danger [in men]?" (p. 82). Tess says that ladies can learn about the possibility of seduction from novels but she had no such education. Joan Durbeyfield defends herself, stating that she thought Tess would be cold with Alec and lose her chance of marriage if she had been warned. Tess's innocence can be seen as part of her downfall.

PHASE THE SECOND, CHAPTERS 13–15

Summary

- Tess feels guilty and ashamed. Friends visit her and she goes to church but she is embarrassed by the congregation's gossip, so then only ventures out at dusk.
- It is harvest time and Tess goes binding (tying the wheat into sheaves). At lunchtime she feeds her baby and the other labourers talk about her sympathetically.
- She enjoys the work and companionship, and her 'moral sorrows' (p. 92) begin to fade.
- Her child, however, is becoming very ill. She is worried that he will be damned because he has not been baptised. Fearful for his soul, she baptises him herself. She names him Sorrow and he dies in the morning.
- The clergyman assures her that Sorrow's soul is safe, but says he cannot permit the baby to be buried on consecrated ground. Sorrow is buried and Tess tends his grave.
- Time passes and, as Tess reflects on her life, she comes to understand her mortality. She decides to go somewhere where she can start afresh.

Analysis

Tess in control

Tess seems to shape her own narrative for a while. She sees herself as a fallen woman, in direct opposition to the narrator, who says that she is innocent according to the laws of nature. Her ability to merge with the environment, and her special relationship with the light of dusk – and later, dawn – are recurring motifs. This section focuses on Tess's thoughts and feelings, sets up the terms for the next section and ties up the second phase. Time and Tess's movement into adulthood are both represented by the passage of the seasons. Tess is once again linked with nature's progress.

Progress booster: Controversial Hardy **(A03)**

The issue of bastardy is touched on here, an ongoing social question for the Victorians, and this coupled with the religious content of the chapter made it deeply controversial. It had to be edited out of the *Graphic* edition. What might Hardy have hoped to achieve as a novelist by courting controversy?

Key quotation: Dairymaid Tess **(A01)**

At the end of Chapter 15 Tess readies herself to move on to the next phase of her life. She needs to shed the recent past: 'On one point she was resolved: there should be no more D'Urberville air-castles in the dreams and deeds of her new life. She would be the dairymaid Tess, and nothing more' (p. 100). She is attempting to take the future into her own hands, to be practical and earn her own money. There is value, pleasure and even the potential for freedom in being just 'the dairymaid Tess'. However, we soon see that the past cannot be annihilated as she hopes; it will always haunt her.

(A05) KEY INTERPRETATION

For an analysis of Victorian literary heroines' relationship to spiritual practices, and Tess's inarticulate – almost animalistic – spiritualism in particular, see Diana Basham, *The Trial of Woman: Feminism and the Occult Sciences in Victorian Literature and Society* (Macmillan, 1992).

(A03) KEY CONTEXT

Cyrus McCormick's horse-drawn reaping machine was displayed in 1851 at the Great Exhibition and was subsequently widely adopted by farmers, thereby largely displacing the work of human reapers and harvesters who, though they no longer used sickles or scythes for cutting, nonetheless still had to bind the corn by hand. Hardy's ambiguous attitude to modernity can be found in his description of the work being done by the mechanical reaping machine, which results in the death of 'Rabbits, hares, snakes, rats, mice ... under the teeth of the unerring reaper, and ... the sticks and stones of the harvesters' (p. 87). See Zena Meadowsong's essay on 'Thomas Hardy and the Machine' in *Nineteenth-Century Literature*, University of California Press, 2009.

KEY INTERPRETATION   (A03)

Jeff Nunokawa argues that Hardy's descriptions, such as his description of 'the valley of the Great Dairies' (p. 102), frequently present the reader with the kind of spectacle more commonly found in nineteenth-century tour guides. See his 'Tess, tourism, and the spectacle of the woman' in Linda M. Shires, ed., *Rewriting the Victorians: Theory, History and the Politics of Gender* (Routledge, 1992).

KEY CONTEXT   (A03)

When discussing Angel Clare in their room at night, one of the girls mentions that he is a parson's son. Reverend Mr Clare is said to be 'the earnestest man in all Wessex, they say – the last of the old Low Church sort' (p. 113). The Low Church was the evangelical branch of the Anglican Church, where worship was characterised by very little ceremony and by a concentration on preaching. The High Church, established by the Anglican 'Oxford movement' (1833–45), revived the ceremonies and rituals of the early Church, and set up Anglican religious communities.

PHASE THE THIRD: THE RALLY, CHAPTERS 16–17

Summary

- Two to three years after her return from Trantridge, Tess leaves home to work as a milkmaid at Talbothays. She is now a woman of twenty.

- As soon as she reaches the valley of the Great Dairies, her spirits rise and she is moved to song. It is milking time and she follows the cows to Talbothays.

- Tess introduces herself to the master-dairyman and sets to work. The cows seem reluctant to give down their milk, so the milkmaids and men begin to sing. Someone suggests that one of the men should play his harp and Dairyman Dick tells a story about William Dewy, who played his fiddle to get away from a bull.

- Tess recognises the owner of the harp as the man who did not dance with her at the club-walking. When she goes to bed, the other milkmaids tell her about Mr Angel Clare, a clergyman's son who is learning about farming.

Analysis

Pathetic fallacy and the landscape

Tess's feelings are often reflected by her environment. It is 'a thyme-scented, bird-singing morning in May' (p. 101) when Tess leaves home for the second time. The pleasant valley echoes Tess's new-found happiness, which resonates in the lush surroundings and bright May sunshine. Looking down on the valley Tess is described as being 'like a fly on a billiard-table of indefinite length' (p. 105), making her seem minuscule in comparison to the scale of the landscape, both in terms of its size and its seeming permanence.

The scene seems timeless, but it is clear that the landscape is, and always has been, in flux, 'compounded of old landscapes long forgotten' (p. 108), while the fact that William Dewy – a character from *Under the Greenwood Tree* (1872) – is buried in Mellstock churchyard gives added depth to Hardy's Wessex. Music, in the form of song, continues to be an important theme.

Revision task 3: Tess's faith   (A03)

Consider the interplay of faith and doubt in nineteenth-century literature, with particular reference to *Tess of the D'Urbervilles*.

- How have Tess's experiences with Alec, and Sorrow's death, affected her faith in God?

- Do Tess's faith and Angel's scepticism make their relationship problematic?

PHASE THE THIRD, CHAPTERS 18–19

Summary

- We are introduced to Angel Clare, who has rejected the key tenets of his father's Anglican faith. Instead of becoming a parson like his father and brothers, Angel is gaining experience in order to become a gentleman farmer.
- Angel now lives in the attic of the dairy and eats with the dairyman, his wife and the labourers, whose 'companionship' he takes 'a real delight in' (p. 117).
- He notices Tess and begins to herd the cows so that Tess gets the easiest ones to milk. She hears Angel playing his harp and becomes fascinated.
- He is puzzled by her bitterness; she is confused by his interest in farming. As time passes, they get to know each other better.

Analysis

Tess and Angel's love affair

This section establishes the terms of Tess and Angel's relationship. They idealise each other – he sees her as a simple 'daughter of the soil' (p. 126), she sees him as an 'intelligence' (p. 125). The references to Tess's difficulty in describing her experiences, the spirit of the age and 'the ache of modernism' (p. 124) are suggestive of Hardy's interest in modernity. But we also see how Tess is subject to nature's rhythms. She is described animalistically, first as a bird then as a cat. The garden's red stains, sticky profusion and clouds of pollen – echoing the clouds of dust in the barn in Chapter 10 – are symbolic of abundant fertility, desire and insemination.

The information that Clare had an affair with a woman in London, and the image of the dairyman's knife and fork being poised like gallows, pave the way for Chapters 34 and 59 respectively. Clare's first observation of Tess – 'What a genuine daughter of Nature that milkmaid is!' (p. 120) – is also ominous.

Study focus: Tess as clairvoyant **A03**

Tess speaks almost as a clairvoyant here: "I don't know about ghosts," she was saying; "but I do know that our souls can be made to go outside our bodies when we are alive" (p. 120).

There was considerable interest in mysticism and spiritualism in the latter half of the nineteenth century among the educated, artistic and professional middle and upper-middle classes, both as entertainment and as philosophy. One of the most famous mediums and founder of the Theosophical Society, Madame Blavatsky, died in 1891. Followers of theosophy included Annie Besant, the social reformer and leader of the 1888 'Match Girls' Strike'; believers in spiritualism included Arthur Conan Doyle and Elizabeth Barrett Browning. Critics included George Eliot and Robert Browning.

A05   KEY INTERPRETATION

Marjorie Garson suggests in *Hardy's Fables of Integrity: Woman, Body, Text* (Clarendon Press, 1991) that the sultry description of nature in the garden is only effective because the sexual nature of Angel and Tess's relationship is otherwise repressed.

A04   KEY CONNECTION

We often find allusions to other texts in *Tess*. As in the previous chapter, in Chapter 18 we find Hardy recycling some of his own work, in this case his essay 'The Dorsetshire Labourer' in *Longman's Magazine* (1883). In the essay, and in this passage of *Tess*, he uses 'Hodge' as a generic name for an uneducated agricultural worker. He would later write a poem entitled 'Drummer Hodge' in which this figure of the generic labourer becomes a low-ranking soldier killed and buried anonymously while serving the British army in the Second Boer War (1899–1902). Sympathy for those at the lower end of the social spectrum was a touchstone of Hardy's writing.

KEY CONTEXT **A03**

Angel is planning on taking on a ten-thousand-acre colonial cattle farm and therefore needs a practical wife. It was relatively common for the younger sons of the well-to-do to invest and become involved in livestock farming in Australia, Canada, the United States and South America in the nineteenth century.

PHASE THE THIRD, CHAPTERS 20–1

Summary

- Tess is very happy at the dairy. She and Angel often meet before sunrise when they go out to milk. He calls her Demeter and Artemis (mythological figures), while she insists that he call her Tess. They begin to fall in love.
- While the dairyfolk wait for the butter to form, they speculate that someone is in love, and dairyman Dick tells a story about a young man, Jack Dollop, who had to hide in the churn to avoid his prospective mother-in-law. Tess is deeply affected by the story and reminded of her past.
- That evening she overhears the other dairymaids talking about Angel Clare. Tess believes that she should never marry, yet she is drawn into thinking about the possibility.

Analysis

Textual echoes

This is a brief, but dense and highly suspenseful section. Hardy reminds his readers of earlier scenes – of Tess's relationship with Alec. His use of figures from classical myth, such as the Greek goddesses Artemis and Demeter, parallels his earlier description of the Chaseborough folk dance. The fog and dewdrops on her lashes echo the scene in The Chase and, because they are described as 'diamonds' and 'pearls' (p. 131), simultaneously foreshadow the moment in Chapter 34 when Tess tries on the Clare family jewels. Although Alec and Angel are very different men, Hardy uses these textual echoes to suggest that the interactions of both men with Tess are dependent upon conventional understandings of gender relations.

Real or ideal?

Tess is idealised by Angel to the extent that, echoing her comments in Chapter 18, she becomes less and less real for him; 'a soul at large', she metamorphoses into 'a visionary essence of woman' (p. 130). Tess has clearly fallen in love with Angel, yet we are reminded, just as Tess is, of the impossibility of living up to an imagined ideal of femininity. We also see the difficulty she faces in attempting to tell Angel about her past sexual experience and thus shatter his idealised image: 'ought she to do this?' (p. 138).

A03

Progress booster: Adam and Eve

The dawn, which stands poised on the threshold between night and day, reflects the way Tess and Angel's relationship is also poised and about to change. The potential for an Edenic fall is highlighted by the reference to Adam and Eve. The Christian idea of 'original sin', and the complexity of Tess's moral position in respect of this, is in turn indicated through the narrator's reference to Mary Magdalene. Think about the ways in which Hardy might be questioning the binary opposition of 'virgin' and 'whore' or Madonna and Mary Magdalene through the figure of Tess.

PHASE THE THIRD, CHAPTERS 22-4

Summary

- At the dairy the butter has a tang of garlic and everyone has to go out to pull up the offending weed. Tess uses the opportunity to divert Clare and get him to look at the other dairywomen.

- It is now July. The dairymaids are all on their way to church, but it has been raining and 'the result of the rain had been to flood the lane over-shoe to a distance of some fifty yards' (p. 142). Angel finds them stranded and carries each one across.

- He and Tess establish an understanding. At first the other dairymaids are jealous, but when Tess tells them that she cannot marry him, the women are reconciled.

- Clare, mesmerised by Tess's beauty, betrays himself by suddenly embracing her: 'Resolutions, reticences, prudences, fears, fell back … and … [he] went quickly towards the desire of his eyes' (p. 151). He stops short of a kiss, but declares his love.

Analysis

Self-sacrifice or desire?

Chapter 22 is a very carefully written chapter which generates a feeling of tension and suspense, reflecting Tess's increasing anxiety about her relationship with Clare. Tess lives up to the Victorian feminine ideal of self-sacrifice here by attempting to interest Angel in her friends. But we are reminded that she is also sensitive to sexual needs and desires. The sentence 'Angel Clare had the honour of all the dairymaids in his keeping' (p. 141), in other words, they would all have offered themselves to him if he had asked them to, becomes pertinent later.

A03 KEY CONTEXT

Attending church or chapel was a way in which young people could legitimately socialise at this time, and it was the one day of the week when they could dress up. Hence Hardy's observation that Sunday is a 'day of vanity … when flesh went forth to coquet with flesh while hypocritically affecting business with spiritual things' (p. 142).

Study focus: Narrative tension   **A02**

Consider how Hardy creates and maintains tension in Chapters 23 and 24. Notice the insects trapped in their skirts and the drip, drip of the cheese press. The oppressive heat tells us a great deal about the nature of Angel and Tess's love. Oppressed by the atmosphere, Angel is also 'burdened inwardly by a waxing fervour of passion for the soft and silent Tess' (p. 149). Angel and Alec are represented as opposites – when Angel is cheek to cheek with Tess he restrains himself. Clare's love is cultured, restrained, even in the heat of passion, unlike Alec's. The embrace takes place in the middle of the day at the height of summer, in contrast to the midnight scene in The Chase – a scene that is echoed by Tess's tears.

Revision task 4: Gender constructs   **A02**

To what extent does *Tess of the D'Urbervilles* suggest that masculinity and femininity are cultural constructs? Make notes on:

- Moments where the concept of 'ideal' femininity is questioned or undermined
- Moments where the attitudes of Angel and Alec are brought into comparison

In Chapter 25, Hardy uses a quote from Walt Whitman's *Leaves of Grass* (first published 1855) to explain Angel's expectation that his life at the dairy would be one of observation more than action: 'Crowds of men and women attired in the usual costumes, / How curious you are to me! –' (p. 153). Whitman's interest in the body, sexuality and nature comes through strongly in his poetry and chimes with Hardy's own interests. Like Hardy's *Tess*, Whitman's work was controversial when first published.

When Angel returns from his parents house he asks Tess about her faith. She doesn't know what type of Christian she is – Evangelical, Tractarian, High, Low or Broad (different modes of Protestant worship). Angel interprets her beliefs as essentially pantheist. Pantheism is a **metaphysical** and religious position which sees God in everything, or more precisely believes that 'God is everything and everything is God' – see H. P. Owen, *Concepts of Deity* (Macmillan, 1971, p. 74) – and which perceives everything as unified, and this unity as being divine.

PHASE THE FOURTH: THE CONSEQUENCE, CHAPTERS 25–7

Summary

- Clare contemplates the consequences of his actions and decides to talk to his family. On the way he meets Miss Mercy Chant, whom his parents want him to marry.
- When he reaches the vicarage he feels that he no longer fits in: 'A prig would have said that he had lost culture, and a prude that he had become coarse' (pp. 158–9). Angel talks with his parents about marrying Tess.
- His father accompanies Angel on the way back to Talbothays, and talks to Clare about his ministry, and how he has often been insulted; once, 'a young upstart squire named D'Urberville' (p. 166) publicly denounced him.
- That afternoon Angel proposes to Tess as they work in the dairy. Tess says she cannot become his wife because of the differences in their station.
- Angel distracts her from her distress by recounting the story of his father and Alec D'Urberville. This reminds Tess about her past and guarantees her second refusal.

Analysis

Focusing on Angel

Chapter 25 focuses entirely on Angel Clare, his motivations and feelings. The narrator gives us a greater understanding of Angel's family background and his father seems more generous and forgiving than his brothers, a fact which is reiterated in Chapter 40. The chapter as a whole lays the ground for Angel's responses and actions later in the novel. Angel's life at Talbothays is in striking contrast to that of his family; the natural life of the farm is opposed to the cultured life of the vicarage.

Reminders of an absent Alec

We already know about Mr Clare's preaching near Trantridge from Chapter 12 and the affair between Clare's father and Alec is picked up in Chapter 45; the legend about the coach is explained in Chapters 33 and 51. The reference to Alec reminds us of the past and **foreshadows** later events.

Study focus: Animal imagery (A02)

Chapter 27 contrasts sharply with the previous two chapters. Tess is described animalistically, like a 'sunned cat' (p. 169) for example. Animal images like these emphasise both her physicality and sexuality. The interior of her mouth is described as snake-like – and Hardy again draws on the story of Adam and Eve: 'she regarded him as Eve at her second waking might have regarded Adam' (p. 170). Note how the narrative focuses on the redness of Tess's mouth when she yawns, and the way the sun catches her veins and penetrates the depths of her hair. The vividness of the narration aligns the reader with the perspective of a lover aware of every detail of the beloved's body, or perhaps a scientist viewing a specimen at the zoo.

PHASE THE FOURTH, CHAPTERS 28–30

A03 KEY CONTEXT

In the late nineteenth century, demand for milk in urban areas remained high. Between 1860 and 1900 annual national consumption rose from approximately 600 to 830 million gallons, and individual consumption rose from nine to fifteen gallons a year. This allowed farmers in dairying counties like Dorset to use the improved communications of the Great Western Railway to offset agricultural depression.

Summary

- Tess's simple charms are contrasted sharply with the flirtatious urban women Clare already knows, yet she is becoming more cultured as she associates with him.

- Tess's conscience continues to make her resist Angel. She says she will give him her reasons that Sunday. Angel proposes again.

- When he kisses her arm Tess, unequal to this moral struggle, runs away to a small wood and misses the milking. She fears that she will give way but refuses again.

- On Sunday morning dairyman Dick returns to the story of Jack Dollop, first mentioned in Chapter 20. He has, among other things, married a widow for her fifty pounds a year, which she promptly lost by marrying him. This leads to the comment by Mrs Crick that 'the silly body [Jack Dollop's wife] should have told him sooner that the ghost of her first man would trouble him' (p. 179). Tess is thrown by this, so does not tell Angel her story.

- A fortnight goes by. Then, after refusing him again, she finally admits to Clare that she loves him.

- Angel and Tess drive the milk to the station. On the way, they pass an old manor house that belonged to the D'Urbervilles. Tess tries to tell Angel her story but falters, and she finally accepts his proposal.

Analysis

Seasonal cycles

Tess and Angel's relationship blossomed and matured as spring became summer, they courted at dawn and now at the autumn equinox everything hangs in the balance. Their desire seems to be part of the natural world in which they live and work. Angel woos Tess among the brooding and farrowing animals and his desire for her leads him to pursue her, almost as Alec did.

A02

Progress booster: Narrative parallels

This is another turning point in Tess's life; many earlier events are recalled and future incidents **foreshadowed** in this chapter. Tess and Angel talk about the stars, as Tess and her brother had done in Chapter 4. The drive is reminiscent of her ride with Alec and her journey at night with Prince. They pass the manor house where they will spend their honeymoon and where Angel will find out that Tess is not as childlike as he thought. The striking image of the train has parallels with the threshing scene in Chapter 47. The engagement takes place at dusk and, though Tess fails to narrate her story to Angel, we remember it all too well.

EXTRACT ANALYSIS: CHAPTER 30, PAGES 186–8

> From 'They crept along towards a point' to 'I was born at so and so, Anno Domini –'

This passage comes almost midway through *Tess of the D'Urbervilles*. It is late summer and Tess Durbeyfield has been working for some time at Talbothays Dairy. Since she has been working there she has fallen in love with Angel Clare. He is the son of a parson but, having abandoned his father's beliefs, hopes to become a farmer. Just before this passage begins, Angel Clare has offered to take the milk to the station with Tess in order to seek her hand. He has already proposed to her, but she has resisted his approaches because she does not feel worthy of him due to her previous involvement with Alec D'Urberville.

KEY INTERPRETATION **A05**

Consider what an **ecocritical** reading of the novel might say about the changes that humans have wrought on the natural landscape. The landscape through which Tess journeys often seems completely natural but we should remember that centuries of agriculture have shaped it into its current form. Here, we see the railway penetrating the rural idyll. How might the coming of the railway affect both the countryside and its inhabitants?

The passage is initially characterised by a description of Tess and Angel's journey to the station, in which Hardy shows the dependence of the countryside upon urban markets and modern technology. It is in passages like this that we can see the degree to which Hardy is preoccupied with the modern. The strangeness of 'modern life' is suggested in the **metaphor** of a 'feeler' stretching out across the countryside (p. 186). Tess is captured and put on display by the light of the steam engine as if she were a scientific specimen. The modern world does not perceive Tess as a personality, she is simply one of the 'native existences' it finds 'uncongenial'. Tess is deeply affected by the experience, as we learn from the simple conversation that takes place when she and Angel move off again. She is visually reduced to the basest, most vulnerable, physical level by the train, but remains 'receptive' to what it represents.

In the past, Tess has resisted Clare when he offered to teach her about history, because it was 'best … not to remember that your nature and your past doings have been just like thousands' and thousands', and that your coming life and doings'll be like thousands' and thousands' (Chapter 19, p. 126). In this respect Tess rebels against the determinism that shapes her life and expresses the 'ache of modernism' (Chapter 19, p. 124) that Angel cannot understand.

The language in the passage shifts between a distanced, abstract narration which uses words like 'feelers' in reference to a simple railway track, and a more immediate narration of the thoughts and feelings of Tess and Clare, from their **point of view**. Tess is not as articulate as Clare; his education shows through in his confident use of language and contrasts sharply with her own clumsy attempt to express what she is thinking. She handles history badly, mixing 'centurions' (p. 187) in with nobles, even though she has been picking up 'his vocabulary, his accent, and fragments of his knowledge' (Chapter 28, p. 175).

Angel teases Tess for this, but the dialogue is disjointed as he constantly interrupts. He is fixed in his determination to pursue his own argument to its logical conclusion and he makes it clear that he will brook no refusal; she will not stand in his way. Angel is a character who cannot alter his mind once it is made up; he is quite unbending and often seems to be just as coercive as the villainous Alec D'Urberville.

Tess is represented here as modest and unassuming, but, as she stands like 'a friendly leopard at pause' (p. 187), we understand that she is intelligent, complex and passionate, even if she cannot always express these aspects of her personality. Angel does not see her animal, 'impassioned' nature, however, only his 'unsophisticated girl'. Because of this rather one-sided view of her, he cannot believe that her 'history' might be a serious impediment to their marriage and he makes fun of her attempt to tell it. Later on in the novel, in Chapter 35, he remembers that he prevented her from confessing, but by that point no longer sees her as the woman whom he is in love with in this passage, his innocent and child-like 'Tessy'.

A05   **KEY CONNECTION**

Take a look at Edna St. Vincent Millay's 'I, being born a woman and distressed' (1923) in the AQA poetry anthology. This poem concerns female sexual desire. Compare the attitude of the female speaker in this poem to Hardy's representation of Tess as an 'impassioned woman'.

Key quotation: A 'well-read woman'   **A01**

Angel responds enthusiastically when Tess tells him of her ancient lineage as a D'Urberville. He says that it will help society to accept her as his wife 'after I have made you the well-read woman that I mean to make you' (p.189)

Although Tess certainly wanted a better education (and we have heard earlier in the chapter that she could have been a teacher if her family had squandered less money), this statement works against Angel's ideal visions of her. It suggests that his love for her is not blind to social considerations and that he assumes that Tess will effectively move up the class hierarchy under his tutelage.

Revision task 5: Visual distance   **A02**

There is a sense of visual distance in much of Hardy's writing.

- Make notes on how the narrator's distance from the action creates a sense of **pathos**.
- List the moments in the text where Tess seems reduced in scale, as if seen from a great distance, or from a God-like perspective.

KEY CONNECTION

Consider the ways in which time moves at a different pace for lovers than it does for other people. Think about the final lines of 'To His Coy Mistress' in the AQA poetry anthology: 'Thus, though we cannot make our Sun / Stand still, yet we will make him run.'

KEY CONNECTION

Angel and Tess's visit to town in Chapter 33 culminates in the altercation brought about by the stranger's recognition of Tess. Hardy used the same setting in 'At an Inn' (see the AQA poetry anthology). In the poem Hardy presents the reader with a pair of lovers who are mis-read by strangers and beset with ill-fortune in their love affair.

PHASE THE FOURTH, CHAPTERS 31–3

Summary

- Tess writes to her mother, who advises her not to confess her past. Tess heeds this advice but has many moments of misgiving.

- The engagement continues through October and Angel insists on setting a date for the wedding. The last day of December is set.

- Tess and Angel spend Christmas Eve together. While they are in town, a man recognises Tess and passes comment. Angel hits him, but events are smoothed over and they return home.

- Angel chooses the old D'Urberville manor house for their honeymoon, on the pretext that he can then visit a neighbouring mill.

- Tess resolves to tell him about her past in a letter but, when the wedding day arrives, she discovers that he never received her confession, 'owing to her having in her haste thrust it beneath the carpet as well as beneath the door' (p. 211).

- They are married and Tess is blissfully happy, but as they leave a cock crows – a bad omen.

Analysis

Time passes

Chapter 32 is a fast-moving chapter. There is a sense of undue haste, and Tess 'was now carried along' (p. 203). The fleeing transitions of time and nature, as seen in the passing glory of the gnats, are highlighted. Clare is acting quite recklessly, and he knows it. Tess's fears, alongside her sense of fatalism, add to the tension. These fears are not unfounded and Chapter 31 warns us that Angel is probably not as forgiving as Tess thinks. The dangers of the excessive idealisation of the Other to which both Tess and Angel succumb are highlighted as the couple speed towards marriage.

Chapter 33, by contrast, is a doom-laden chapter in which Tess is beleaguered by omens, including the spectre of the D'Urberville coach from Chapter 26, much reduced like the family itself. The focus is as much on the grotesque as it is on the happy event.

Study focus: Joan's voice

Chapter 31 begins with Joan Durbeyfield's letter to her daughter advising her against revealing her past: 'why should you Trumpet yours when others don't Trumpet theirs?' (p. 191). Joan's voice is very distinctive and her written words echo her vernacular speech very closely. The sentiment of her advice is practical and pragmatic and she compares Tess with her father by using the same word – 'simple' – to describe them both. The fundamental attitudes of Tess and Joan are oppositional but it is important to recognise the effect that Tess's mother has on the plot here and at other turning points in the novel.

PHASE THE FOURTH, CHAPTER 34

Summary

- Tess and Angel drive to the manor at Wellbridge to start their honeymoon.
- As they go up to their rooms they see the life-size portraits of two D'Urberville ladies and feel discomfited by their resemblance to Tess.
- While they wait for their luggage Tess tries on some jewels left to Clare's wife by his godmother. Angel is impressed but says he prefers her in her working clothes.
- The boy who brings their luggage tells Tess and Angel that Retty has tried to drown herself, Marian is drunk and Izz is depressed. This news makes Tess determined to confess.
- Angel tells Tess of an early misdemeanour and she now feels confident enough to tell him her story.

Analysis

A sisterhood of sorrow

The Talbothays dairymaids, Izz, Marian and Retty, have all reacted badly to the marriage of Tess and Angel and the loss of their beloved. The messenger says, 'It seems as if the maids had all gone out o' their minds' (p. 222). Retty's attempt to drown herself turns the scale for Tess and precipitates her confession. It is the personal sorrows of her friends, rather than an abstract sense of duty, that finally leads to Tess's confession.

Creating suspense

The chapter moves back and forth between description and dialogue, which generates considerable suspense. The consequences of Tess's confession are hinted at in the description of the lurid fire, by the shadow which she casts and by the way in which she seems to be taking up the mantle of the D'Urberville women. The phase ends on a cliffhanger as Tess starts to reveal her past.

A trencher was originally a kind of bread used as a plate, on which cut meat was served. It was probably only used in the medieval period at feasts, when several fresh trenchers would be needed for elaborate meals. They would be pre-made for important guests, but trenchers could also be cut as thick slices from ordinary loaves as needed. A 'trencher-woman' (p. 222) as used here is a woman who eats meat, or a stout woman.

A02

Progress booster: Mirroring and doubling

Notice how Angel and Tess seem to almost blend together at certain moments in this chapter. Angel enjoys touching her hands as they wash together and eating from the same plate as his new wife. As Angel begins his confession Tess thinks, 'He seemed to be her double' (p. 224). The proximity of these lovers is poignantly undermined when Angel judges Tess's sexual past more damningly than his own. The doubling of their stories highlights the double standard that Hardy seeks to reveal at work in his society.

PHASE THE FIFTH: THE WOMAN PAYS, CHAPTERS 35–6

Summary

- Tess finishes her confession.
- Angel is horror-stricken and no longer sees Tess as the woman, nor as the 'new-sprung child of nature' (p. 232), he loved; she can say nothing to console him. When he goes out she follows him and they walk slowly around the village until he tells her to return to their lodgings.
- When Angel gets back he is reminded of Tess by the portraits of the D'Urberville women. They sleep in separate beds.
- In the morning Angel goes to work at the mill and the next three days pass quietly.
- Tess hopes that Angel will forgive her, but it gradually becomes apparent that he cannot and she suggests that she return to her family.
- Angel observes that he is likely to love her better in her absence.

Analysis

Gothic elements

The ruined abbey symbolises the decline of conventional morality, but this **Gothic** detail also adds to the feeling that Angel is haunted by the spectre of his simple 'Tessy', grotesquely transformed into the sinister aristocratic paintings of the D'Urberville women. When they are seen walking by a local cottager he sees them as if 'in a funeral procession' (p. 233). Even Angel himself is affected; his laugh is 'as unnatural and ghastly as a laugh in hell' (p. 228).

Study focus: Intensified perceptions

Look out for subtle details like Angel's tear which 'magnified the pores of the skin over which it rolled' (p. 230). The narratorial voice is intently focused on the two lovers in this section. Think also about the ways in which ordinary objects, like the fire and the fender, seem to be transformed by Tess's confession.

Imperfect lovers

In Chapter 36 both Tess's and Angel's faults are considered. The fact that their affection differs is stressed and this echoes what was said about the nature of their love towards the end of the last phase. However, Tess's purity is maintained by the narrator – she is not artful or sophisticated enough to manipulate Angel – and the possibility that he will return to her is hinted at. Does she get the idea of murdering Alec from Angel's suggestion, 'If he were dead it might be different …' (p. 243)?

KEY CONTEXT **A03**

Civil divorce courts were established in England and Wales with the Matrimonial Causes Act 1857, which also gave women custody rights for the first time. However, women only had limited access to divorce; although a husband could apply for divorce on the grounds of adultery, a wife could only do so on the grounds of her husband having committed bigamy, rape, sodomy, bestiality, cruelty or desertion. Divorce was also expensive and still limited to the wealthy; only 582 people had divorced by 1900.

PHASE THE FIFTH, CHAPTERS 37–9

Summary

- Angel, sleepwalking and murmuring 'Dead! dead! dead!' (p. 246), carries Tess out into the night and lays her in a stone coffin in the ruined abbey. Tess leads him back without waking him. He remembers nothing the next day. He gives her fifty pounds, tells her not to write and they part as planned.

- Tess returns home, but on the way is embarrassed to hear the story of her own marriage. Her mother reprimands her for confessing and when she overhears her father doubting the validity of the ceremony she decides to leave as soon as possible.

- When a letter comes from Angel, in 'her craving for the lustre of her true position as his wife, and to hide from her parents the vast extent of the division between them' (p. 258), she pretends they are reconciled, gives her mother half of the money Angel has left her and goes.

- Three weeks after the separation, Clare goes back to Emminster. He has decided to emigrate and tells his parents that he has left Tess with her family while he visits Brazil.

Analysis

Melodramatic moments

Chapter 37 is a highly sensational chapter marked by exciting incidents and strong uncomplicated feelings. Tess's life is in danger for much of this chapter, from the moment where Tess is balanced on the bannister of the house to the terrifying crossing of the fast-flowing river. Unlike a **melodramatic** text, however, it does not have a happy ending.

The changes in Tess and Angel's relationship are reflected in the turbulent waters of the river and are highlighted by the memories conjured up when they visit the Cricks. The pity and sadness that are aroused, and the **pathos** of Tess being put in the abbot's tomb, prefigure her and Angel's arrival at Stonehenge in Chapter 58 and seem to play on eerie **Gothic** motifs.

Middle-class morality

In Chapter 39, the narrator highlights the class bias of Angel's parents. We see how, despite Angel's supposed rejection of social custom and his own very sensuous memories of Tess, his conventional expectations of a woman's sexual morality come out of his family background. The moral of the novel is addressed and, with particular stress being placed on Tess's purity, a clear authorial position emerges: 'In considering what Tess was not,' we are told, 'he overlooked what she was, and forgot that the defective can be more than the entire' (p. 265).

A02

Progress booster: Returning home again

Note how Tess's second return home in Chapter 38, similar to that in Chapter 12, creates a symmetrical structure in the novel. At home, Tess drops Angel's more cultured language. While her parents are selfish, Tess is full of pride, as we were reminded in the last chapter. Consider Tess's interactions with her family and community and the decisions Tess makes. Is her pride part of her downfall?

A03 **KEY CONTEXT**

Read 'La Belle Dame sans Merci' by John Keats in the AQA poetry anthology. It too features a sleep-walking lover and compares a dream love to the withered, waking reality.

A03 **KEY CONTEXT**

Cattle ranching was slower to become established in Brazil than in neighbouring Argentina or Uruguay due, among other factors, to less suitable soil, lack of sufficient railroads, a shortage of foreign investors and limited local capital. The industry did not therefore take off until the late nineteenth century, and potential settlers had to be attracted via financial incentives such as cheap land and passage.

PHASE THE FIFTH, CHAPTERS 40–2

Summary

- While sorting out his affairs Angel meets Mercy Chant. He deposits thirty pounds for Tess's use and writes to tell her to contact his family if she is in need.
- When Angel re-visits Wellbridge to pay his bills, Izz Huett, from Talbothays, appears. He offers her a lift home and asks her to go to Brazil with him. She agrees, but when she says that no one could have loved him more than Tess did, he abandons her.
- Eight months later, Tess has used up all her allowance. She does not want to ask for more money and sets out to join Marian, also from Talbothays dairy, on another farm, Flintcomb-Ash.
- As she travels she is accosted by the man who insulted her in Chapter 33. She hides in a wood. During the night she hears wounded pheasants dying and falling from the trees. In the morning she kills them. We are told that Clare is unwell in Brazil.
- Tess finally arrives at Flintcomb-Ash.

Analysis

Angel and Izz

Angel is tempted to fall into Alec's evil ways and seduce Tess's friend from the dairy. When deeply distressed, he is morally inconsistent. Izz is described as 'an honest girl who loved him – one who would have made as good, or nearly as good, a practical farmer's wife as Tess' (p. 268) but she admits she could never love Angel more than Tess. Notice the contrast between Izz Huett and Mercy Chant. Angel's attempt to take up with Izz Huett, a woman from the same background as Tess, prefigures his relationship with Tess's sister in Chapter 59.

Dramatic narration

At times in these chapters the narration moves from past to present tense. For example, the phrase 'Thus Tess walks on; a figure which is part of the landscape; a field-woman pure and simple, in winter guise' (p. 280) reads almost like a stage direction. Similarly, when Tess is presented to us in Chapter 41, 'We discover the latter in changed conditions' (p. 272). The idea of 'discovering' a character on stage refers to the raising of the curtains to find them in position. Hardy might be considering Tess as an actor here, enacting a pre-ordained plot.

Progress booster: Tess and natural life **A02**

In Chapter 41 Tess seems like a wounded animal, comparing the birds' suffering to her own. The season, as always, reflects the mood of the narrative and Tess's progress through her short life. Chapter 42 begins by focusing on Tess's feelings, but draws back to reveal a new, barren landscape. Consider how an **ecocritical** approach would illuminate the relationship between Tess and the natural world. She often seems in harmony with nature, she takes nothing from the landscape through which she walks, but sometimes the environment seems to conspire against her. The weather is getting colder and the landscape more barren as she makes her way to Flintcomb-Ash.

KEY CONTEXT **A03**

By the late nineteenth century it was commonplace for landowners to run commercial shooting parties. Pheasants and grouse were bred for the purpose by gamekeepers, while boys and men would be hired by the day as beaters to flush the birds towards the gunmen. It would have been unusual to leave birds wounded and Tess quickly puts an end to their suffering. The use of land for game was a point of contention between farmers and landowners, as the game (it was argued) destroyed crops. Taking the birds illegally (poaching) was a serious offence.

PHASE THE FIFTH, CHAPTERS 43–4

Summary

- Tess's work on the farm is hard and her employer is the man who insulted her in Chapter 33.
- When Marian and Tess work in the fields they can just see Talbothays; this prompts them to talk about the past. Marian is drinking and Tess still hopes that Angel will return.
- Izz Huett joins them as they work in the barn with the Queen of Spades and her sister, the Queen of Diamonds.
- When Tess hears of Angel's proposition to Izz she starts writing to him, but cannot finish.
- Tess decides to see Angel's family, fifteen miles away. Just outside the town she changes out of her walking boots and leaves them in the hedge.
- While waiting for Mr and Mrs Clare she overhears a conversation between Angel's brothers. They are talking about Angel 'throwing himself away upon a dairymaid' (p. 300) as they pass her.
- Angel's brothers and Mercy Chant find Tess's boots and take them for a needy cause.
- Disheartened, Tess gives up and walks back to Flintcomb-Ash.
- On the way she stops to hear a preacher and is surprised to see that it is Alec D'Urberville.

Analysis

Anthropomorphism and dehumanisation

Hardy describes the women's field work in detail, but also likens the landscape to the human form. This **anthropomorphic** treatment suggests that Hardy is not simply concerned with the scrupulous representation of the women's employment or of human nature; things are not presented as they are, so the chapter is much less **realist** than it appears. The women are dehumanised by the work, 'their movements [showing] a mechanical regularity' (p. 285), but their concerns and experiences are equally reduced by the immaterial, transcendental or **metaphysical** power of nature, as represented by the passage of nameless arctic birds, silent witnesses to grotesque, unimaginable horrors.

Study focus: Chances missed

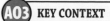

Chapter 44 brings the phase to an end by providing Tess with her last real chance of help from Angel, and by reintroducing Alec. The unfortunate coincidences of missing Angel's parents whilst they are at church, of overhearing Angel's brothers, and of losing her boots give a sense of opportunities narrowly missed and events conspiring against Tess. This adds to the **pathos** of her failure. Notice the bloodied piece of paper that blows up and down outside the vicarage, and the painter of signs in Alec's congregation – both also signs of Tess's inability to escape her tragic fate.

Whereas working with poultry, in a dairy or in a harvest field were all deemed 'respectable' forms of employment for rural women, field work was not. Reports in the 1860s on women's and children's work in the fields argued that it was physically and morally corrupting. Contrastingly, Hardy's descriptions of field work have often been likened to the semi-impressionist rural paintings of the artist George Clausen (1852–1944), who founded the New English Art Club in 1866.

The poor in the nineteenth century were deemed to be either 'deserving' or 'undeserving' by those in a position to help them. The 1834 Poor Law Amendment Act was designed to ensure that no one would seek aid from a workhouse unless they had no other choice, and private charities were careful to select those they helped on the basis of good, moral behaviour. Begging, or vagrancy, was meant to be strictly controlled by law. Mercy Chant and Angel's brothers are very unsympathetic when they imagine a morally suspect vagrant to have left their boots in the hedge in order to enter Emminster barefoot and gain charitable handouts.

PHASE THE SIXTH: THE CONVERT, CHAPTERS 45–6

Summary

- Tess is at first shocked by the sight of Alec preaching, then quickly leaves.
- Alec sees her, falters in his preaching and catches her up. He tells her that he was converted by the Reverend Mr Clare after Mrs D'Urberville died.
- Tess does not believe that Alec has changed, and compares him to Angel, who has rejected his father's faith.
- Just before leaving her Alec makes her swear, on what he thinks is a cross, that she will not tempt him. A shepherd tells Tess that the 'Cross-in-Hand … a strange rude monolith … on which was roughly carved a human hand' (p. 310) is really an ill-omened memorial.
- Alec visits Tess while she is working and asks her to go with him to Africa as a missionary's wife.
- She tells him that she cannot marry and he gleans a little of her circumstances. When they are interrupted by the farmer Alec defends Tess from his insults.
- Tess tries again to write to Angel, but again she fails.
- The others go to a hiring fair and Alec visits Tess while she is alone. They discuss Angel's doctrinal views and Alec tells her that by visiting her instead of preaching he has fallen.

Analysis

Alec's conversion

Tess is shocked by Alec's conversion, as is the reader. We are told that 'animalism had become fanaticism' (p. 305) and even Alec's appearance has altered in the light of his new-found faith. The reader may have trouble believing in Alec's conversion and the narrator points out the 'incongruity' (p. 305) of the words of scripture coming from Alec's mouth. Tess generously accepts his conversion at this point, although she is still fearful of him.

Parallels between Alec and Angel

Alec has apparently taken up elements of Angel in the way that Angel took on aspects of Alec in Chapter 40. The theological discussion in the cottage in Chapter 46 holds Angel and Alec in tension. It is Angel's words, spoken by Tess, that undo his father's conversion and make Alec lose his faith. There are also parallels between the two men in the idea of emigration, and in Alec's threatening Tess's employer. Both Angel and Alec contemplate taking Tess abroad. Like Angel earlier, Alec now becomes Adam to Tess's Eve; the suggestion is that he will fall to her temptation.

PHASE THE SIXTH, CHAPTER 47

Summary

- It is March and the last wheat rick has to be threshed by a steam-driven threshing machine.
- The work is unremitting and Tess is chosen for one of the hardest tasks: untying the sheaves so that the corn can be fed into the hopper.
- Alec, who has now lost his faith and his morality, appears while they break for lunch and offers to take her away.
- She hits him with her glove and makes his lip bleed.
- Alec leaves, but promises to return.

Analysis

Machine as metaphor

The threshing machine is given human qualities and made to seem in control of the scene. Perhaps it is representative of the mechanistic law of fate that seems to be directing Tess's life towards a tragic end. It has also been read as a symbol of the agricultural revolution which has swept away the old relationships of the countryside, so that men like Alec, who do not care about or understand their obligations, now stand in the place of old feudal families such as the D'Urbervilles, who had a more organic relationship with the land and its people. The monstrous threshing machine can be compared to the blood-red reaping machine in Chapter 14 and the train in Chapter 30, which also have metaphorical significance.

A changing Tess

We could argue that this chapter demonstrates a change in Tess's character. For example, we are told that she 'had gathered from Angel sufficient of the incredulity of modern thought to despise flash enthusiasms' (p. 329), and Alec comments that he has seen her change. An unsympathetic reading of Tess could suggest that when she strikes Alec she gets a taste for his blood that is really only satisfied when she murders him in Chapter 57.

Revision task 6: The impact of modernity **A02**

Hardy chose a rural idyll for his setting, but in what ways does modernity impact on rural life in his novel? Consider any moments:

- When machines enter the narrative
- Where time itself seems to speed up in the narrative

A05 **KEY INTERPRETATION**

A Marxist interpretation of Chapter 47 would be interested in the way that the farm workers are dehumanised by their work with the threshing machine and alienated from the products of their labour. Farmer Groby treats his workers as wage slaves, getting the most labour out of them for the least payment.

A02 **PROGRESS BOOSTER**

Note how the threshing machine is described as 'the red tyrant that the women had come to serve – a timber-framed construction, with straps and wheels appertaining'. We are told that whilst it is running it 'kept up a despotic demand upon the endurance of their muscles and nerves' (p. 325). The machine rules over the scene here and speeds up the rhythms of rural life. The intensity of Tess's work on the machine takes a physical and an emotional toll on her.

KEY CONTEXT   **A03**

KEY CONTEXT   **A03**

Mrs Clare worries that Angel has been 'ill-used' (p. 338) as he was not sent to university like his brothers because of his religious doubts. Her implicit criticism is that Angel's life would not currently be in danger in Brazil if he had been allowed to take a more conventional path in life. Until the passing of the University Test Act in 1871, all academics and students at Oxford and Cambridge universities had to be regular Anglican churchgoers. This act opened the universities to all faiths based on ability.

PHASE THE SIXTH, CHAPTERS 48–9

Summary

- The threshing continues into the evening and Alec returns as promised. The rats that run out of the last sheaf are hunted down and the work finishes.

- Alec and Tess seem to be reconciled after their earlier altercation. He offers to help her and her family, but again she refuses any aid.

- At the end of the day Tess feels troubled enough to write to Angel and plead for him to return. Tess's letter is sent on to Angel via the vicarage.

- Angel has been ill and, influenced by a stranger, now regrets his treatment of Tess. While away he has 'mentally aged a dozen years' (p. 340).

- Meanwhile, Tess waits for Angel's reply and practises singing the ballads he liked.

- Just before Tess's time on the farm is up, 'Liza-Lu appears and asks Tess to go to their mother and father.

- Tess leaves her sister to catch up the next day and sets off home.

Analysis

Study focus: Building tension   **A02**

Notice how tension builds in Chapter 48 as Alec continues to pursue Tess, as if she were one of the rats which emerge at the end of the threshing. Tess is again likened to a wounded animal, this time a 'bled calf' (p. 335). Alec goes after her when she is at her weakest, and the offer to help her family is aimed at her most vulnerable point. Does comparing Tess to an animal in this way reinforce her lack of control over her life?

Tess's letter

It is interesting to see how Tess's letter to Angel moves backwards and forwards between hope and despair. In deep distress, she writes to him showing that she understands the consequences of Alec's snares and implying that Angel's prolonged silence is unfair and may be more than she can bear. Earlier, Angel had suggested that Tess was an 'an unapprehending peasant' uninitiated in 'the proportions of social things' (Chapter 35, p. 232). Her letter suggests that she actually has a very clear apprehension of her social situation and its difficulties. The letter presents one of the few occasions in which Tess is apparently given her own voice.

A new Angel?

In Chapter 49 we follow Tess's letter into the vicarage and then on to Brazil, where Angel comes back into focus. Angel tells a well-travelled stranger about his disastrous marriage and to the traveller's 'cosmopolitan mind' (p. 341) Tess's past seems insignificant. It is a stranger in a strange land, outside of the usual social norms, who can tell Angel that he has treated Tess badly. Angel's inner psychology is revealed to us and we see how the separated lovers are continually in each other's thoughts.

PHASE THE SIXTH, CHAPTER 50

Summary

- It is over a year since Tess was last at home. She helps her mother to recover and sets about planting up the garden and allotment with her father.
- One evening, she finds Alec D'Urberville working beside her on the allotment.
- Again, he offers to help her family and again she refuses his aid. When Tess returns to the house she finds that her father has died.
- Because the lease on the cottage ends with her father's life, her family will have to leave the cottage and find a new home.

Analysis

Tess returns home again

This is Tess's third and final return home. Once again she is walking alone, this time in darkness. The world feels unreal, the landscape reflects her history, which is mingled with its own, and her perceptions are changed just as they were when she went walking at night in Chapter 13. We get a sense of her vivid inner life as she imagines the 'relaxed tendons and flaccid muscles' of those sleeping inside the houses she passes and identifies strongly and emotionally with her family home as soon as she sees it (p. 345).

Devilish Alec

Alec's sudden reappearance by firelight, holding a pitchfork, reminds us of his devilish aspect, which is reinforced when he calls her Eve and names himself 'the old Other One' (pp. 348–9). This is reminiscent of Chapter 45, in which Alec made Tess swear on a stone that commemorated a man who had sold his soul to the devil, but it also brings together the imagery of fire – for instance, her confession in Chapter 34 – and of the Fall, in which she has been figured both as Eve and the snake. These images have pursued Tess throughout the novel.

(A02)

Progress booster: Rhythms of fate

There is a reference to a kind of natural justice in the family's removal from their cottage, a fatality in the idea that the once powerful D'Urberville family are now at their lowest ebb. The narrator finishes Chapter 50 with 'So do flux and reflux – the rhythm of change – alternate and persist in everything under the sky' (p. 351).

What kinds of rhythms are represented in the novel? Consider the daily rhythms of farm life, seasonal rhythms, the cycles of generations and even the flux of geological time – all are present in the text. How do they impact on Tess's story?

(A03) KEY CONTEXT

Social reformers argued throughout the nineteenth century that agricultural labourers should be provided with some ground, e.g. a garden, allotment or 'potato ground', on which they could grow food. A similar argument was made about those who lived and worked in the towns. In 1887 the Allotment Act required authorities to supply allotments if there was a demand.

PHASE THE SIXTH, CHAPTERS 51–2

Summary

KEY CONTEXT **A03**

Hardy comments on the social changes caused by the movement of rural families from small villages towards larger towns. There was a housing shortage in rural areas throughout the nineteenth century. Most cottages were 'tied', i.e. provided as part of a labourer's hiring agreement, and would therefore have to be given up as soon as the labourer changed jobs or lost work. In the Victorian era there was no safety net provided by the government and if the family could not find themselves work and accommodation the workhouse would await them. Victorian workhouses were grim places, families were usually separated and often some form of forced labour had to be undertaken.

KEY CONNECTION **A04**

See Hardy's poem 'The Ruined Maid' for a satirical take on the relative position of women who maintain their moral worth and those who don't.

PHASE THE SIXTH, CHAPTERS 51–2

Summary

- Tess's family have to leave their home. They have arranged lodgings in Kingsbere.
- Alec appears while Tess is alone in the cottage. He offers to give her and her family shelter in the garden-house where she worked at Trantridge.
- She turns him down again and he rides off. Suddenly angered by her situation, Tess writes Angel a short, angry note.
- On the way to Kingsbere the Durbeyfields stop at an inn, where Tess exchanges news with Marian and Izz.
- Just before the family reach their new lodgings, they are told that the arrangement has fallen through. The driver drops their furniture off at Kingsbere church and Tess's mother makes up a bed by the south wall, near the D'Urberville tomb.
- Tess is frightened by Alec, who rises from one of the tombs in the church and again offers to help. She sends him away, and wishes she were dead.
- In the meantime, Izz and Marian wonder if they can help Tess; a month later they write to Angel, who is on his way back to Britain.

Analysis

Omens and consequences

Chapter 51 sees what is left of the Durbeyfield family sliding further down the social scale. Tess's history is placed in its social context, so that we see the material consequences of an ostensible loss of purity given that 'the [Durbeyfield] household had not been shining examples either of temperance, soberness, or chastity' (p. 352). Tess blames herself for her family's misfortunes, as she did when their horse died. When Alec relates the story of the D'Urberville coach, it works both as an omen within the narrative, and prefigures Tess's actions in the next phase. The 'man with the paint-pot' (p. 356) reappears: he symbolises both moral boundaries and their transgression. Again, Tess speaks through a letter, this time impassioned, but still well written. The children's Sunday-school song adds **pathos**.

Gothic motifs

Chapter 52 sees **Gothic** motifs juxtaposed with the banalities of the Durbeyfields' ramshackle journey with their household goods. When Tess sees the d'Urberville vaults she asks herself 'Why am I on the wrong side of this door!' (p. 364). Alec, who has assumed the D'Urberville name, springs from the family tomb.

Key quotation: 'They were only women' **A01**

A feminist interpretation of this section would consider the social injustice to which Tess, her mother and their family are exposed merely because they are women. We are told, 'They were only women … they were not particularly required anywhere' (p. 358). Their labour is undervalued and they are exposed to social, and sexual, danger. Despite the fact that the patriarch of the family was improvident, without him the Durbeyfields face even greater difficulties.

PHASE THE SEVENTH: FULFILMENT, CHAPTERS 53–5

Summary

- The Clare family are shocked by Angel's appearance when he returns.
- He has received Tess's plea for help and now he reads her rebuke. He hesitates to go to her because of this and writes instead.
- He gets a reply from Joan, who says Tess is away, she cannot say where. After rereading Tess's letters, and the one from Marian and Izz, Angel decides to find her.
- Eventually he arrives at Joan's cottage. Joan finally lets him know that Tess is at Sandbourne, a fashionable resort. Angel immediately catches the last train there.
- Early the next morning, he finds her, considerably altered in dress and manner, staying at a lodging house under the name Mrs D'Urberville.
- She tells him that Alec helped her family and therefore managed to win her round. She says that Angel's return has come too late and, though she now hates Alec, she insists that Angel leave.

Analysis

Detective plots

With Angel's efforts to trace Tess, a detective plot enters the narrative at the end of the novel. The reader is placed in a position of ignorance, like Angel, creating a feeling of suspense. We move through the process of tracing Tess with him. Detective stories had become very popular in the late nineteenth century. Charles Dickens is often said to have introduced the first detective with Inspector Bucket in *Bleak House* (1852–3) but many other novels, such as Mary Elizabeth Braddon's *Lady Audley's Secret* (1862) used the figure of the amateur detective to unravel a mystery or find a missing person. Hardy was aware of the detective plot and expectations of the form, such as searching for a missing person under multiple aliases.

Sandbourne: an alien landscape

The description of Sandbourne (Hardy's name for Bournemouth) in Chapter 55 highlights how this is an alien landscape for Angel and Tess: it is a 'pleasure city' and a 'glittering novelty' (pp. 375–6) sprung up amidst the rural landscape. When Angel takes lodgings in Sandbourne, he asks himself, 'Where could Tess possibly be, a cottage-girl, his young wife, amidst all this wealth and fashion?' (p. 376).

Absent Tess

Tess is absent from the narrative until we near the end of Chapter 55. Angel has had to retrace her steps and walking in her shoes seems to have awakened his sympathies all the more fully. However, even when we do see our protagonist again, the Tess we know seems to have gone. Alec's name goes unsaid, but he has fulfilled his promise to dress her 'with the best', as he said he would in Chapter 12 (p. 77). Her clothes heighten her 'natural beauty' (p. 378) and her hands are no longer reddened as they once were from dairy work. Finally mastered by Alec, Tess is no longer herself; her spirit and her body are no longer as one.

A03 KEY CONTEXT

In the Victorian period it was assumed that a woman's clothes reflected not only her class and social position, but also her moral standing. Prostitutes were, for instance, said to typically dress in 'finery' – lace, feathers, satins and velvets – such finery suggesting that they were dressing above their station and, when tattered, connoting their moral impropriety. See Elsie Michie, 'Dressing Up: Hardy's *Tess of the D'Urbervilles* and Oliphant's *Phoebe, Junior* in *Victorian Literature and Culture* (2002).

A02 PROGRESS BOOSTER

Look at Hardy's use of mirroring in his choice of language. When Angel returns to Emminster, his parents 'could see the skeleton behind the man, and almost the ghost behind the skeleton' (p. 368). Angel is like a ghost returned to life, but he is also haunted by his own past, particularly his unfair treatment of Tess.

PHASE THE SEVENTH, CHAPTERS 56–7

Summary

- Mrs Brooks, the landlady of Tess's lodging house, follows Tess upstairs, listens at her door and looks through the keyhole.
- She overhears Tess's lament, but retreats in fear of being discovered.
- Later, she sees Tess leave and, later still, looks up to see a growing red stain on the ceiling. She gets a workman to open the door and Alec is found dead in bed. The alarm is raised.
- On checking out of his hotel, Angel receives a message that one of his brothers has become engaged to Mercy Chant.
- Angel goes to the railway station but, tired of waiting, decides to walk on to the next.
- Tess catches him up and tells him she has murdered Alec in order to be free again.
- Angel is not sure if this is actually the case, but decides to protect her. Dazed, they walk on into the countryside and find shelter in a deserted house.

Analysis

Through the keyhole

Chapter 56 provides us with glimpses of Tess's reaction to Angel's return, through Mrs Brooks's perspective. She peeks through the keyhole and sees Tess's despair. Narrating this scene through the perspective of a minor character provides us with some relief from the emotional intensity Tess is feeling, while retaining the **pathos** of the situation. It also means that Hardy does not have to show Tess committing murder, which may have made it more difficult to retain the reader's sympathies for her. The chapter does contain detail that is almost surgical – the knife just clips Alec's heart – and reads like a court testimony. This detachment, coupled with Mrs Brooks's **point of view**, generates a sense of suspense.

Tying up loose ends

Chapter 57 ties up several loose ends and plot points prefigured in earlier passages. Tess hit Alec with her gauntlet in Chapter 47, thus, by her own admission, **foreshadowing** the murder. Angel can love Tess now that Alec is dead, as he said he might in Chapter 36. Tess says she killed Alec after he called Angel 'a foul name' (p. 385) – Angel hit Farmer Groby for a similar offence to Tess in Chapter 33. Notice too the return of the D'Urberville coach and further reference to the depravities of the decayed D'Urberville blood that contaminates Tess's veins.

PROGRESS BOOSTER **A02**

Angel and Tess wander reborn like babes in the wood in Chapter 57 – Tess is 'at last content', while tenderness is 'absolutely dominant in Clare at last' (p. 385). In what ways is this idyll shown to be fleeting?

PHASE THE SEVENTH, CHAPTERS 58–9

Summary

- Tess and Angel stay in the empty house for a number of days, protected by a dense fog. Finally, someone comes to air it and sees them sleeping.
- They wake and flee, and finally come across Stonehenge in the darkness.
- Tess is tired and they rest. She asks him to marry 'Liza-Lu, who 'has all the best of me [Tess] without the bad' (p. 394). Angel is unable to say that they will meet in heaven.
- As Tess sleeps the police arrive; they arrest her when she wakes.
- Time passes and it is July when we see Angel and 'Liza-Lu walking up a hill out of Wintoncester in the early morning. They stop as the clock strikes eight and watch the prison which they have just left.
- They see a black flag raised as Tess is hanged, they appear to pray, then move on.

Analysis

Tess's acceptance of her fate

We no longer see Tess as struggling against her tragic fate. Stillness pervades Chapter 58. Once they find shelter in the deserted house she does not wish to move further in an attempt to evade the police. She accepts that justice will come and admits to Angel: 'I do not wish to outlive your present feeling for me' (p. 390). There is considerable narrative play between rapid movement across great tracts of land, and stillness, while Tess and Angel hide. Hardy employs quite complex yet **naturalised** dialogue to give Tess her last chance to speak.

'The heathen temple'

It is fitting that a novel which has wrestled with the difficulties of belief in a benevolent Christian God should set a final scene at 'the heathen temple' (p. 393) Stonehenge. When Tess suggests that Angel marry 'Liza-Lou after her death she feels she could share her beloved Angel with her sister when they are spirits. Tess assumes the existence of an afterlife here, but when she asks Angel his opinion he cannot reply, he silently kisses her.

A02

Progress booster: Symbolism of the sun

The sun has been a significant motif throughout the novel and here Tess is sacrificed in an ancient temple dedicated to the sun, Stonehenge. Key moments in Tess's life have often happened either when the sun is setting or rising. Consider where else in the novel Tess is associated with the sun, and what this association might connote.

A03 **KEY CONTEXT**

According to ecclesiastical law, based on the biblical teaching of Leviticus and reinforced in 1848, a man could not marry his sister-in-law; for example, if his wife was deceased the husband could not then marry his dead wife's sister. This only changed once the Deceased Wife's Sister Bill was finally passed in 1907.

Finality and detachment

The final chapter is narrated at a distance, with complete detachment. Tess's execution is placed within the context of the fate that marked her at the outset of the novel and with reference to the tombs of the D'Urbervilles. 'Liza-Lu is an innocent version and 'a spiritualized image' (p. 396) of Tess – in other words, the idealised woman Angel loved all along.

EXTRACT ANALYSIS: CHAPTER 59, PAGES 396–8

> From 'One of the pair was Angel Clare' to 'they arose, joined hands again, and went on.'

This passage belongs to the final chapter of *Tess of the D'Urbervilles*. By this point Angel, who initially deserted Tess because of her affair with Alec D'Urberville, has learned to forgive her. While Angel is abroad, Tess has to support herself by working in the fields at Flintcomb-Ash. During this period she attempts to get help from Angel's family, and on her return runs into Alec, who claims to be converted. He soon loses his faith and begins to pursue her again. When her father dies, and convinced that Angel will never come back, she consents to live with Alec. When Angel finds her living with him she is devastated; she kills Alec and runs after Angel. They hide, but after sharing a few brief days of happiness, Tess is finally arrested at Stonehenge.

The novel ends in movement, as it began; Angel and 'Liza-Lu move mechanically like Tess's father did in his drunken journey home from market in Chapter I. The whole scene is written with detachment, so that we know nothing of Angel's and 'Liza-Lu's feelings as they watch 'Justice' being done; they do not speak, or think, they just act. As with the scene on The Chase, we do not see the actual violence committed against Tess, which is when her blood is, in a sense, first spilled, but we do overhear a degree of **ironical** authorial intervention. The indifference of 'the D'Urberville knights and dames' continues (pp. 397–8). It is as if Tess has never lived.

We see images that have been closely associated with Tess throughout the novel – the prison is built of 'red-brick', the midsummer sun shines brightly – but she is represented by a new sign, 'a black flag'. Tess is brought to a standstill while her husband and her sister, who has her 'beautiful eyes', walk on. Much of the description is indeterminate, for instance Angel and 'Liza-Lu kneel '*as if* in prayer' [my italics], while the infinite spread of 'landscape beyond landscape' is dizzying. The sentences are long, but straightforward, adding to the impression of a long view. Here Hardy slips into a tourist-book style with a touch of Latinism in which he draws on his architectural training to describe Wintoncester's buildings, 'as in an isometric drawing' (p. 397).

We do not know if Angel and 'Liza-Lu marry, of course, but the fact that they walk off hand in hand suggests that they do. So, although this is the final chapter of the book and the theme of fate, or the inevitability of history, seems to conclude in the phrase 'the President of the Immortals … had ended his sport with Tess', this new relationship, described in the present tense, resists completeness and finality, or **closure**, in the text. The heroine is absent; what we actually see is 'Liza-Lu stepping into her place as 'a spiritualized image of Tess', ready to repeat the ancient history of the D'Urbervilles.

PROGRESS CHECK

Section One: Check your understanding

These tasks will help you to evaluate your knowledge and skills level in this particular area.

1. In what ways is Tess disadvantaged by her background? Make a list of four or five reasons outlined early on in the novel.

2. Make a table contrasting rural life with the modern world as it is glimpsed in the novel.

3. List four or five moments in the narrative that shed light on the character of Angel Clare.

4. Consider two or three of the minor characters in the novel and list their functions in terms of supporting the development of the plot or the development of other characters.

5. List three or four significant social changes Hardy examines in the novel and consider how they effect rural life.

6. What is the significance of machines in *Tess of the D'Urbervilles*? Give at least two examples.

7. Identify three of Tess's solitary journeys and briefly consider the significance of each.

8. Make a table offering points of comparison between Angel and Alec. Think about both similarities and differences.

9. Write a paragraph on what you find interesting about the depiction of the natural environment in Hardy's novel.

10. Consider three of the letters written in the novel. What are their functions and what do they reveal about their writers?

11. Why are animals significant in this text? Give three examples of different animals used by Hardy.

12. List three moments when the narration becomes distanced or detached and think about why Hardy might adjust the perspective of the novel at key moments.

13. List three instances of violent action in *Tess of the D'Urbervilles* and comment on each.

14. How is love represented in the novel? Write a paragraph considering imagery, symbolism and dialogue.

15. Make a table listing three or four events that happen in the second half of the novel and the ways in which they are foreshadowed in the first half.

16. How is the impact of rural depopulation felt in this novel? Make a list.

17. Think about the three key families in this novel: the Durbeyfields, the Clares and the D'Urbervilles. Make a table outlining contrasts and comparisons.

18. Why is work so significant in this novel? Write a short paragraph explaining your answer.

19. List four or five ways in which the present is haunted by the past in Hardy's novel.

20. Consider the moments in the novel where we are invited to think about families and heredity. List both the positive and negative qualities that might have been passed down to Tess through her family.

Section Two: Working towards the exam

Choose one of the following five tasks which require longer, more developed answers. In each case, read the question carefully, select the key areas you need to address, and plan an essay of six to seven points. Write a first draft, giving yourself an hour to do so. Make sure you include supporting evidence for each point, including quotations.

1. *Tess of the D'Urbervilles* is a story about the relationship between the individual and their hostile environment. Discuss.
2. Does Hardy's novel criticise inequality? If so, how and why?
3. How far do you agree with the idea that Tess's fate could only ever be tragic?
4. How is the novel's concern with the passage of time reflected in its structure?
5. What is the relationship between religion and morality in *Tess of the D'Urbervilles*?

Progress check (rate your understanding on a level of 1 – low, to 5 – high)	1	2	3	4	5
The significance of particular events and how they relate to each other					
How the major and minor characters contribute to the action					
How Hardy plays with narratorial perspective					
How Hardy structures the narrative					
The final outcome of the story and how this affects our view of the protagonist					

CHARACTERS

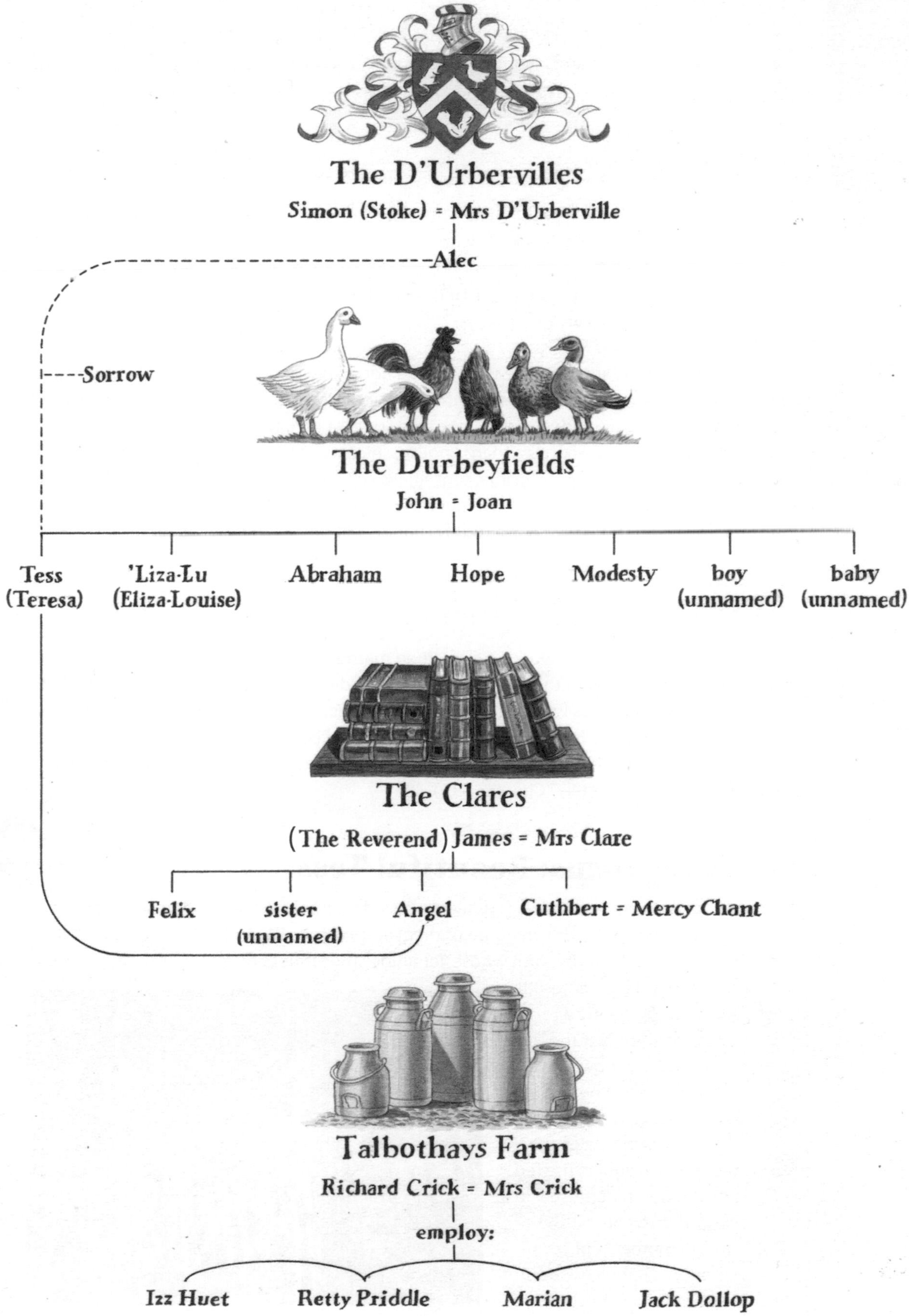

The D'Urbervilles

Simon (Stoke) = Mrs D'Urberville

— Alec

- - - Sorrow

The Durbeyfields

John = Joan

| Tess (Teresa) | 'Liza-Lu (Eliza-Louise) | Abraham | Hope | Modesty | boy (unnamed) | baby (unnamed) |

The Clares

(The Reverend) James = Mrs Clare

| Felix | sister (unnamed) | Angel | Cuthbert = Mercy Chant |

Talbothays Farm

Richard Crick = Mrs Crick

employ:

| Izz Huet | Retty Priddle | Marian | Jack Dollop |

Tess

Who is Tess?

- Tess is a beautiful young woman who has always lived a rural life.
- She is raped by Alec and later married to Angel, and eventually hanged for Alec's murder.
- Hardy presents Tess as a figure of psychological complexity and modernity.

A complex woman

Tess originally presented a problem for critics because of her 'purity'; today, it is still all too easy to see her as a real person who is independent of the text. Tess of the D'Urbervilles, a pure woman, is, however, a complex fictional character who is used by Hardy to represent the insoluble social ills of his day. Because of this complexity it is possible to read her, and therefore the novel, in a variety of ways.

First of all it is important to realise that Tess is a figure in whom oppositions like virgin and whore collapse; she is not one thing or the other, but both. Both 'unapprehending peasant' (Chapter 35, p. 232) and educated woman, she speaks two languages – the dialect of her home and an educated Sixth Standard English; she acts according to nature, but is sensitive to social convention; the passive innocent, she is still, in part, proud and responsible for what happens to her; a victim, she is also a murderer. We cannot tell what she is just by looking at her, and the novel is structured around the dangers of misreading her as Angel and Alec do.

A figure of modernity

Tess initially belongs to the working class, then marries above her station. This representation of social mobility is part of the modern condition and reflects the period in which the novel was written. Because Tess is a modern rather than a Victorian character we, as modern readers, can identify with her. We find the novel painful because she feels the 'ache of modernism' (Chapter 19, p. 124), is impotent and inconsequential, and is the plaything of the 'President of the Immortals' (Chapter 59, p. 397).

KEY CONTEXT **A04**

Tess of the D'Urbervilles is like a medieval morality play, a **psychomachea**, in which Angel and Alec – the former representing virtue and the latter vice – seem to fight for the soul of Tess. Our understanding of each of the characters therefore depends, in part, on their relationship to the others in the novel.

Study focus: Beautiful Tess **A01**

Notice how our eye is always drawn to Tess. Among the other binders she is 'the most flexuous and finely-drawn figure of them all' (Chapter 14, p. 88); it is her work which is described in detail, her arm whose 'feminine smoothness becomes scarified by the stubble, and bleeds' (p. 88). Angel is apparently wrong to idealise Tess, yet the text itself sets her above the other women of her class. We are asked to note that 'The cheeks are paler, the teeth more regular, the red lips thinner than is usual in a country-bred girl' (p. 89). And, in moments of emotional intensity, she seems to move beyond the bounds of ordinary, everyday life.

Animalism

Tess is not always elevated; she is also represented as belonging to nature. We are often given the impression that she communes with the animal kingdom and on these occasions she seems to be more animal than human. Tess is sympathetic to the wounded pheasants in Chapter 41; she is likened to 'a bled calf' in Chapter 48 (p. 335); and as her captors catch up to her at Stonehenge, 'her breathing now was quick and small, like that of a lesser creature than a woman' (Chapter 58, p. 395). Her animality is used to make her appear vulnerable, but also to highlight her sexuality.

Progress booster: Always a pure woman

Hardy did not condemn Tess for her baser animal instincts, or for having had an illegitimate child, of course; she remained 'a pure woman' in his view, as the subtitle to the novel makes clear. The problem for contemporary critics was that purity equated with virginity. When Tess is suddenly pitched from the pedestal of natural beauty into the mire of sexuality in The Chase, Hardy shows how women are wronged by the standards of his day. She was the exception that Hardy created to prove the rule. A heterogeneous figure, her society could not comprehend or forgive a woman who was neither virgin nor whore, but contained aspects of both.

A05 KEY INTERPRETATION

Gemma Arterton's portrayal of Tess in the 2008 BBC mini-series allows us to compare Tess's simple dress and innocent rural attitude in its first instalment with the very differently attired Tess Angel finds at Sandbourne. The screenwriter, David Nicholls, also picks up on the symbolism with which Hardy portrays Tess.

Key quotation: Tragic Tess

Talking to Angel before they are married, Tess confides that she seems to see 'numbers of to-morrows just all in a line, the first of 'em the biggest and clearest, the others getting smaller and smaller as they stand farther away; but they all seem very fierce and cruel' (Chapter 19, p. 124).

Tess seems to understand that fate is conspiring against her and that her path in life will always be difficult. However, she goes on to tell Angel that he can 'raise up dreams with your music, and drive all such horrid fancies away!', so she still has the capacity for hope and joy. The narrator sees Tess's complex sense of self as part of what makes her modern.

Alec

Who is Alec?

- Alec is a rich, pleasure-seeking young man who does not have to work because he has inherited his father's wealth.
- He is a sexual predator who pursues Tess and rapes her.
- He undergoes a (temporary) conversion to religious faith.

A passionate lover

Alec is the more passionate of Tess's admirers and he responds to Tess erotically from their first meeting when he asks, 'Well, my big Beauty, what can I do for you?' (Chapter 5, p. 40). He rejects the old-fashioned moral standards and social conventions of his day and expects to master Tess as he does his horse. A 'cad' and a sexual predator, he is selfish, arrogant, violent, capricious and superficial. But he is capable of slow seduction as well as domination, and this quality, coupled with his roguish good looks, can help us to understand how Tess becomes beguiled by him. A real moustache-twirling villain from **melodrama**, he can be quite difficult for some readers to believe in.

KEY INTERPRETATION **A05**

Marjorie Garson's *Hardy's Fables of Integrity: Woman, Body, Text* (Clarendon Press, 1991) carries a useful analysis and diagrammatic representation of Tess's relationship with Alec and Angel, and of each man's relationship to the other.

A failed convert

Through Alec's failed conversion, Hardy presents his view of the deterioration of Christianity in the modern world, and this makes the character more complex. It also provides another cross-reference with Angel, as it is Angel's father who first sets Alec on the path to conversion. Ironically, it is Angel's words (repeated by Tess) that cause Alec's religious zeal to fade. The novel shows that Alec can change but the ease with which he slides back to his old persona makes us doubt the depth of his religious conversion.

Progress booster: Mirroring masculinities **A02**

It is important that you can write about how Angel and Alec are played off against each other throughout the narrative: Angel plays a harp (and his name, of course, gives him a sense of the angelic), whilst Alec is presented as devilish. Angel's love is spiritual, Alec's is material. But the two men are not always oppositional: Angel momentarily takes on aspects of Alec's personality when he asks Izz to go with him to Brazil; both men think of taking Tess abroad; Alec loses his new-found faith thanks to Angel's ideas; both are harmful to Tess. Consider how Hardy uses these contrasts and similarities between the two men.

Key quotation: Alec **A01**

Alec has 'an almost swarthy complexion, with full lips … above which was a well-groomed black moustache with curled points' (Chapter 5, p. 40). Alec's full lips are symbolic of his sensual nature and the well-maintained moustache gives us a sense of his vanity. Alec is so full of self-regard that each time Tess rejects his offers he is piqued to try again rather than accept her rejections.

Angel

Who is Angel?

- Angel Clare is a young man from a strongly religious family.
- He rejects his religious upbringing and is training to be a gentleman farmer.
- He loves Tess with an idealising desire and urges her to marry him, only to reject her when she confesses her past.

A man of logic?

Angel is a man of the 1890s who rejects the precepts of Christianity, as we learn in Chapter 18. But he is also an intellectual who falls prey to his emotions. We see from very early on in the novel that he is unlike his college-educated brothers. In Chapter 2, Angel stops to dance with the girls at Marlott whilst his brothers move on discussing theological matters. Even here his emotional sensitivity overcomes his logic and looking back at the unknown figure of Tess he 'instinctively felt that she was hurt by his oversight' in not dancing with her (p. 18). Interestingly, Tess herself is frequently aligned with instinct rather than logic.

An objectifier

Angel looks at Tess as a thing of beauty, he **objectifies** and idealises her, mistaking her for a goddess; he does not love her, as she says, for her *self*. Hardy extensively revised this character, during which process Angel's love became less sensual, and more ideal. However, Angel is also aware of the difference in social standing between himself and his wife and promises to educate and guide her so that she will be more acceptable to his family. Though Angel returns from Brazil to consummate his marriage, he still ultimately takes 'Liza-Lu, who is an idealised version of Tess, in her sister's place.

Progress booster: Is Angel a hypocrite? **A01**

It is easy to read Angel as a hypocrite. At the crucial moment he cannot forgive Tess for her past, despite his own previous sexual experience. However, his near death experience in Brazil helps him to see more clearly the parallels in their experiences and finally, he returns to her, to show the reader how Tess has been wronged by the social conventions of his day. He is the more complex of the two men in Tess's life because he has the more complicated role. It is this character who helps us to fall in love with Tess, but who also demonstrates the cruelty of her **tragedy**.

Key quotation: Angel's idealisation of Tess **A01**

When discussing his future wife with his parents, Angel tells them that Tess will be an 'apt pupil' and adds 'She's brim full of poetry – actualized poetry ... She *lives* what paper-poets only write' (Chapter 26, p. 164). The fact that Angel represents Tess as a poem or a work of art reinforces Angel's dangerous idealisation of Tess. He is also aware that her practical skills as a dairymaid would make her a capable farmer's wife and he does not fail to point out Tess's experience with farm work to his parents.

A04 **KEY CONNECTION**

Consider the Christina Rossetti poem 'Remember' in which the speaker asks their interlocutor to 'Remember me when I am gone away'. Think about Tess's injunction to Angel to marry her sister, 'Liza-Lu. Is this a similarly double-edged command to that seen in the Rossetti poem, to move on but maintain a connection to what has been lost?

A05 **KEY INTERPRETATION**

For an interesting account of the triangulation of desire between Tess, Angel and Alec, see Richard Nemesvari's essay 'Erotic Triangles and Masculine Identity' in *Thomas Hardy: Texts and Contexts* (Palgrave Macmillan, 2002) edited by Philip Mallett.

KEY CONNECTION A04

Consider the minor characters in George Eliot's *The Mill on the Floss*, particularly the protagonist, Maggie Tulliver's, aunts – Jane Glegg, Sophy Pullett and Susan Deane. They provide a foil for the heroine with their banality working against her rejection of social convention. Consider the ways in which the minor characters in *Tess* might also highlight the differences between themselves and the protagonist.

Other characters

Tess's family

Tess's family are poor, but this is mainly because her parents are idle spendthrifts, not because they are peasants, as Hardy makes clear in Chapter 5. Tess's parents are proud and ambitious but profligate. Tess's father is a tranter or small dealer; her mother cares for Tess, 'Liza-Lu, Abraham, Hope, Modesty, 'a boy of three' (Chapter 3, p. 24) and the baby. Tess has aspects of her mother and her father in her, and her family helps us to understand her character more thoroughly. Through them it is also made clear that Tess sees herself as the only industrious and dependable member of the household, and we are shown how Tess comes to take on responsibility for them, which shapes most of her decision-making.

Joan and Jack Durbeyfield

Tess's mother has been seen by some critics as conspiring against her daughter, as setting her up in the hopes of acquiring social, or at least financial, advancement. The text leaves room for doubt: for example, when Joan sees Alec coming to pick Tess up in person she claps her hands in joy but then doubts herself: 'Could she be deceived as to the meaning of this?' (Chapter 7, p. 52). A sympathetic reading of Joan would not suggest that she is purposefully prostituting her daughter.

If Tess's mother offers only equivocal support, her father is even less of a good example for his daughter. Jack is irresponsible with money, deluded about the significance of his ancestry and often drinks too much. The novel opens with him staggering home from market, and it is his drinking that requires Tess to take the horse out on the fateful night it is killed. His feckless ways and large family leave the Durbeyfields in constant need.

Angel's family

Angel's family is not as well defined as Tess's, but various members of the family appear in several chapters. Angel's brothers, 'starched and ironed' (Chapter 44, p. 301), are introduced in Chapter 2, when Angel stops to dance with the village girls at the club-walking. When Angel first visits the vicarage in Emminster, in Chapter 25, we are introduced to his family at breakfast – including his absent elder sister via a portrait. All of them are, in some way or another, involved with the Church. From this chapter we gather that his father is supposed to be admirable and sincere; a staunch Evangelical, his precise sympathies are made known to us through his choice of quotations and his favourite theologians.

All the family evince some difficulty in dealing with or understanding the lower classes, but it is evident from the outset that Angel's brothers are particularly bound by convention in this respect. When Angel invites his brothers to join in the country dance with him in Chapter 2, Felix exclaims snootily, 'Dancing in public with a troop of country hoydens – suppose we should be seen!' (p. 17). Angel's parents are more generous than his brothers, as we are told in Chapters 39, 44 and 53, but they are as limited as Angel himself when it comes to imagining the human complexity of a country maid.

Hardy uses the Clare family to demonstrate his view of the limitations of the English middle class when it comes to morality. It is their class that condemns Tess, of course, and we are much less surprised by Angel's reaction to Tess's confession because we have learned something about his origins.

Substitutes for Tess

Tess plays maternal and sisterly roles in the novel, and the women around her cannot help but feel affection for her. Izz, Retty and Marian, Tess's co-workers at the dairy, do not begrudge Tess Angel's love, despite their own affection for him. Izz in particular functions as a substitute for Tess when Angel asks her to accompany him to Brazil just after their initial separation. She would follow Angel anywhere and break any social code for him but despite her nature being 'rougher' (Chapter 40, p. 270) than Tess's she cannot lie and admits that no one could love him more than his wife.

Tess is upset when she hears about Angel's attempt to substitute her with Izz but late in the novel she attempts her own substitution, asking Angel to marry her sister 'Liza Lu who is 'so gentle and so sweet' (Chapter 58, p. 394). We hear very little from 'Liza Lu herself and she is still very young, but by the final pages of the novel Angel walks away with his sister-in-law who is described as a 'spiritualized image of Tess' (Chapter 59, p. 396).

Study focus: Minor characters

A01

Be aware of the array of minor characters, some of whom appear several times in the novel and add to its highly-structured plot. For instance, the reappearance of the man who paints slogans, whom Tess first meets in Chapter 12, acts to remind us of the moral boundaries which Tess has crossed. These characters range from those who are simply incidental, to those who provide comparative and background material. Hardy uses the rougher characters to hint at a certain vulgarity or essential paganism in country life, while the idealised dairyfolk help construct a rural idyll at Talbothays.

Revision task 7: Angel's love for Tess

A01

Make notes to show how you would support or argue against the claim that Angel loves an ideal version of Tess, not the 'real' character. Consider the moments of their courtship at Talbothays in particular.

A04 **KEY CONNECTION**

The fact that Angel says Tess's 'arms are like wet marble' (Chapter 30, p. 185) implies that he sees in her the embodiment of perfected and **objectified** femininity, and makes oblique reference to the story of Pygmalion. In the story of Pygmalion an artist (Pygmalion) falls in love with a marble statue that he has carved. His love is so strong that the Roman goddess Venus brings the statue to life. This myth was represented by the Pre-Raphaelite Edward Burne-Jones in four paintings entitled *Pygmalion and the Image* (1878).

KEY INTERPRETATION

For a detailed discussion of the extent to which Hardy's representation of rural life was accurate, or rather whether or not it was complete, see K. D. M. Snell's *Annals of the Labouring Poor* (Cambridge University Press, 1987).

THEMES

Loss, inevitability and the passage of time

As Hardy explores the human condition, so wandering, loss and the inevitability of suffering and death become the dominant themes of the novel. Even the simple passage of time is shown, within this context, to be malign. In *Tess*, all the characters, but especially Tess herself, seem to be under the control of an external force that conspires against them – 'the President of the Immortals' (Chapter 59, p. 397).

A tragic inheritance

Tess Durbeyfield is an ordinary country girl, but her life and death are affected by the fortunes of her predecessors, the ancient D'Urbervilles. She is bound to repeat and duplicate what has gone before. Hardy presents Tess as being snared by the past, and doomed from the outset: her death on the gallows seems both inevitable and, given that Angel is able to replace her with 'Liza-Lu, insignificant. Even as she enters the Valley of the Great Dairies, where she will be at her happiest, her position there is likened to that of 'a fly on a billiard-table of indefinite length, and of no more consequence to the surroundings than that fly' (Chapter 16, p. 105). The past, therefore, determines the present, as seen in the landscape, in communities and in individuals' lives.

Progress booster: The inevitability of the past

A01

Note how Tess tries to capture and live just for the present: "'Don't think of what's past!" said she. "I am not going to think outside of now. Why should we! Who knows what to-morrow has in store?"' (Chapter 58, p. 389). In other words, Tess learns to reject both history (Chapter 19) and the future (Chapters 15 and 19). She wants to teach this to Angel, and it is Tess who creates the space, the short period of happiness they have together. She does this, however, by a deliberate act that both makes this period possible and will inevitably bring it to an end – in other words, Alec's murder. Hardy brings us to the conclusion that the individual is never totally free to act, that their life is predestined, that passivity is preferable to wilfulness.

The natural and conventional

The relationship of humanity to nature forms the second major theme of the novel. This is a complex theme within which nature and convention are juxtaposed.

Natural resurgence

Hardy's repeated emphasis on Tess's purity argues the case that the 'recuperative power which pervaded organic nature was surely not denied to maidenhood alone' (Chapter 15, p. 99). Here, Hardy is suggesting that natural life is full of perpetual renewals, such as the movement of the seasons, so why should our attitude to Tess's virginity be any different?

Tess herself takes time to mourn the loss of her innocence and of her baby but she is not broken by this early experience. She takes pleasure in the world around her because of nature and Hardy describes Tess's own resurgence in natural terms: 'some spirit within her rose automatically as the sap in the twigs. It was unexpended youth, surging up anew after its temporary check, and bringing with it hope, and the invincible instinct towards self-delight' (Chapter 15, p. 100).

The cruelties of the natural world

Hardy also presents nature as cruel: 'the serpent hisses where the sweet birds sing' (Chapter 12, p. 75). When Tess arrives at Flintcomb-Ash, the 'stubborn soil showed plainly enough that the kind of labour in demand here was of the roughest kind' (Chapter 42, p. 282). The terriers that catch the rats, the fog that shrouds Alec's rape of Tess, even the garlic that sours the butter are examples of a harsh and unfeeling natural world. Of course, the natural environment is made more difficult by social circumstances, such as Farmer Groby's harsh attitude to his workers or Alec's predatory opportunism.

Study focus: Nature as structure **A02**

Notice how Hardy uses nature in the novel as a presence and as an idea. In the form of seasons it helps add structure to the novel – and to people's lives. It is used as the norm against which characters and situations are judged, and as a pressure or force that acts on the characters: 'A particularly fine spring came round, and the stir of germination was almost audible in the buds; it moved her, as it moved the wild animals, and made her passionate to go' (Chapter 15, p. 99).

Make sure you can write about how Tess's movements around the county often coincide with changes in the seasons or in the weather, and the effect this has on both the narrative and the presentation of Tess herself.

A05 KEY INTERPRETATION

One of the concerns of directors of film adaptations of Tess has been to consider how to situate Tess as part of an environment that seems almost to conspire against her. The setting of a Hardy film needs to be more than just a backdrop to the action. See Peter Widdowson's 'Thomas Hardy at the End of Two Centuries: From Page to Screen' in *Thomas Hardy: Contemporary Literary Studies* (Palgrave Macmillan, 2004) for an interesting essay on a number of film adaptations.

Hardy admitted in a letter that 'I...lost my heart to her [Tess] as I went on with her history'. Do you see any evidence of this statement at work in the novel? Does the narratorial voice harbour any desire for the protagonist? If so, consider what effect this might have on the reader.

Margaret Elvy in *Sexing Hardy: Thomas Hardy and Feminism* uses feminist and **queer theory** to unpack Hardy's understanding of sexual difference and sexual desire. Elvy does not agree with some feminist critics that Hardy has a 'natural' empathy with women. This approach is more interested in the ways in which Hardy's female identities are complex constructions.

Love

Sexual love

We could argue that Tess's two lovers represent different types of love: Alec's love is material and sensual, whereas Angel's is ideal. However, Angel is not immune to Tess's sexual allure. We are told that he 'was driven towards her by every heave of his pulse' (Chapter 25, p. 155) and in almost every scene at Talbothays Angel tries to move close to Tess's desired body. Tess, too, is a sexual being and Hardy's language make the sexual union between the two seem all the more natural. For example: 'Every see-saw of her breath, every wave of her blood, every pulse singing in her ears, was a voice that joined with nature in revolt against her scrupulousness.' (Chapter 28, p. 178)

The love of mothers

Several of Tess's key actions in the novel (seeking out the D'Urberville family, or finally giving in to Alec's advances) are motivated by Tess's love for her family. These actions are self-sacrificing and, in many ways, Tess is fulfilling a mother's role by putting the needs of her younger brothers and sisters before her own. We must also remember that Tess is an actual mother and her conflicted love for her child is manifested in the violent kisses she gives to him alternating with 'gloomy indifference' (Chapter 14, p. 90). Tess's maternal affection for Sorrow continues after his death and we later see her tending the baby's impoverished grave.

Study focus: Forced love

In Chapter 9 we meet Mrs D'Urberville and are told that she 'was not the first mother compelled to love her offspring resentfully, and to be bitterly fond' (p. 60). What other relationships do we encounter in the novel where love seems forced or compelled against the lover's better judgement?

Religion and justice

Spirituality in family life

When we meet Angel's family in the vicarage at Emminster, we see how religion is central to their lives. All of the Clare children have followed religious paths in their lives: one brother is a curate, another is a scholar at Cambridge and Angel's sister is a missionary in Africa. Religious services, family prayers and visits to their parishioners structure his parents' lives. We are told that although Angel 'could not accept his parent's narrow dogma he revered his practice and recognized the hero under the pietist' (Chapter 26, p. 167). Angel's father lives out his religious faith in acts of self-sacrifice like giving away the food and drink Angel brings from Talbothays to a needy family. Although Hardy himself may have had religious doubts, he obviously retains respect for those, like Mr Clare, whose faith is sincere and active.

An Eden on earth

Talbothays is likened to the garden of Eden in the third phase of the novel. We are told that Tess regarded Angel 'as Eve … might have regarded Adam' (Chapter 27, p. 170) and that the two lovers 'seemed to themselves the first persons up of all the world' (Chapter 20, p. 130). The light of the dawn impresses them 'with a feeling of isolation, as if they were Adam and Eve.' These references to Eden make Tess and Angel's courtship seem blissful and almost supernatural but they also hint that this state of bliss will only be temporary. Their happiness at the dairy must come to an end, just as the perfection of paradise ended when Eve gave into the serpent's temptation and tasted the fruit of knowledge.

Progress booster: Justice for women

A01

When the black flag is raised to indicate that Tess has been hanged, the narrator tells us that "Justice' was done' (Chapter 59, p. 397). Think about the use of **irony** in this phrase. Justice may have been done according to a very black and white understanding of justice as a kind of punishment: Tess must be killed because she has killed someone. But we understand that the narrator is actually asking us to question this notion of justice. Nothing about Tess's life has been fair. There was no legal retribution for Alec's rape, nor was there any justice in Angel's reaction to Tess's admission of her past. We might start to wonder whether the notion of justice is a social construct of little use to women like Tess.

Revision task 8: Sexual morality

A03

Examine the theme of sexual morality in the novel. If there is a double standard at work, how might this be interpreted? Make notes on:

● The different attitudes to forgiveness that we encounter in the text

● The significance of Angel's accusation to Tess: 'You were one person; now you are another.' (p. 228)

A02 **KEY INTERPRETATION**

See *Thomas Hardy and the Law: Legal Presences in Hardy's Life and Fiction* (2003) for a discussion of how the novel's interest in sexual desire (particularly Alec's rape of Tess) can be situated in its historical legal context.

PROGRESS CHECK

Section One: Check your understanding

These tasks will help you to evaluate your knowledge and skills level in this particular area.

1. Write a list of four or five ways in which minor characters impact upon the trajectories of the central plot.

2. Locate a passage of dialogue between Tess and Alec and one between Tess and Angel. Compare the ways in which Tess's lovers speak to her and what their conversation reveals about their attitudes to their beloved.

3. 'A weakness of this novel is that neither Angel or Alec are truly believable characters.' Do you agree with this statement? Set your thoughts out in a table.

4. Make a table offering three or four comparisons of the cruelties of nature versus the benevolence of nature.

5. What is the thematic significance of ruined or dilapidated buildings in the novel?

6. How does Tess's story show gender to be a significant issue? List three events and briefly explain the significance of each.

7. Make a list of three ways in which religious faith is problematised in the novel.

8. Identify three types of love found in the novel and give an example of each.

9. Write one or two paragraphs discussing the idea that in the world of the novel justice is possible for men but not for women.

10. Give an example of **pathetic fallacy** in the novel and explain its significance.

PROGRESS BOOSTER   **A01**

For each Section Two task, read the question carefully, select the key areas you need to address, and plan an essay of six to seven points. Write a first draft, giving yourself an hour to do so. Make sure you include supporting evidence for each point, including quotations.

Section Two: Working towards the exam

Choose one of the following three tasks which require longer, more developed answers.

1. Compare the representation of women in *Tess of the D'Urbervilles* with the way in which female characters are presented in any of the other texts you have studied.

2. 'Tess embodies a clash between nature and society.' Do you agree?

3. Discuss the ways in which Hardy's narrator seeks to represent an unequal and unjust society.

Progress check
(rate your understanding on a level of 1 – low, to 5 – high)

	1	2	3	4	5
The key actions, motives and thoughts of major and minor characters in the text					
The different ways you can interpret particular characters' words and actions					
How characterisation is linked to key themes and ideas					
The significance of key themes and ideas within the text					
How some key themes (such as love or suffering) are linked to context					

GENRE

Tragedy

The fact that the novel ends with the protagonist's death aligns *Tess of the D'Urbervilles* very clearly with the genre of **tragedy**. There are many events in the novel that we might call tragic: the death of Prince, Tess's rape, the death of Sorrow. All these more minor tragedies are related to the ultimate tragedy of Tess's hanging. Tess herself often seems to have a tragic or pessimistic worldview. She tells Angel, 'This hobble of being alive is rather serious, don't you think so?' (Chapter 19, p. 123) and tells her younger brother Abraham that their world is 'A blighted one' (Chapter 4, p. 31).

A key element of classical tragedy is the idea of a fatal flaw in the hero or heroine which leads to their downfall. Arguably, for Hardy the fatal flaw in *Tess of the D'Urbervilles* is that of society itself, which fails to protect and support vulnerable women like Tess.

A02

Progress booster: Possibilities for happiness

Note that the tragedy of the novel is often reinforced by glimmers of hope soon dashed. Think about where Hardy locates hope or optimism in the novel and whether any hope remains for the reader at the **denouement**. Consider also the happier paths from which Tess is narrowly diverted by miscommunications or unfortunate coincidences. Think of examples of these moments and consider their importance to the tragic plot.

Naturalism versus realism

Given the emphasis on fate, coupled with the biological and sociological pressures that are placed on the characters, the novel might be categorised as naturalist. **Naturalism** expresses a post-Darwinian view of life in which human beings are seen as fundamentally no more than specialised animals, subject to natural forces such as heredity and the environment. Naturalists see a novel as a kind of experiment and claim a degree of scientific accuracy for their work. Typical subject matter are the miserable and poverty-stricken, or those driven by animal appetites such as hunger or sexuality. Life is viewed as a squalid and meaningless tragedy. Although Hardy does dwell on the difficulties of Tess's life, he is also insistent that Tess as an individual is connected to larger philosophical issues. For Hardy the individual life is meaningful; for naturalists the individual life is ultimately insignificant.

It is also difficult to categorise *Tess* as a **realist** novel. Realists aim to present 'things as they are' and in the nineteenth century most realist novels consisted of a detailed representation of life and depiction of human nature as it really was. 'Realism,' Hardy said, 'is not art.' *Tess* is about isolation and separation, the condition of modernity. We can see Hardy's 'realism' therefore simply as a literary device which helps him to outline Tess's joy, stoicism or humiliation.

A05 KEY INTERPRETATION

Michael McKeon's *Theory of the Novel: A Historical Approach* (Johns Hopkins University Press, 2000) is an excellent introduction to the history of the novel. It provides examples of different ways of understanding the novel form. One of the most useful approaches for Hardy's work is to think about the novel as a genre that has the capacity to critique the society in which it was written.

A04 KEY CONNECTION

Many writers have considered whether realism is possible at all in literature. A writer like Virginia Woolf in *Mrs Dalloway* uses a number of perspectives to emphasise the ways in which we all see the world differently. Our understanding of reality therefore becomes subjective rather than objective.

STRUCTURE

Hardy's phases

The novel is very carefully structured around seven phases. The handling of time relies partly on season, but varies in each phase. We can see a range of temporal scales at work in the novel, including the distant past, the recent past, insect, animal and human time. Apart from this, Hardy often uses very subtle shifts back and forward in time. For instance, when we catch up with Joan and John at Rolliver's in Chapter 4, the narrative moves back in time before moving on to the point where Tess decides to go and collect them at the end of Chapter 3.

On other occasions the narrative speeds on over several years, as at the end of Phase the Second. As we have already seen, it would be all too easy for the novel to fall into two halves because of the way in which Angel and Alec tussle over Tess. This helps explain Hardy's extensive use of reminders, links and cross-references within each phase, but these also add to the overall sense of pattern in Tess's life.

KEY INTERPRETATION **A05**

In *The Nature Novel from Hardy to Lawrence* (Macmillan, 1977) John Alcorn argues that Tess's story is encapsulated by her movement across the land. This text was written before **ecocriticism** had defined itself as a particular method of interpreting texts. However, his work stresses the importance of environment and the potentially damaging relationships between humanity and the landscape, much as later ecocriticism does.

Tess on the move

Tess's journeys provide an alternative structure to the seven phases of the novel. She leaves home four times and returns three times. Each time Tess leaves home – when she travels to Trantridge, Talbothays, Flintcomb-Ash and Sandbourne – she is slightly altered, and this makes each new journey slightly different to the last. She also goes to Emminster, and finally flees to Stonehenge, from which there is no return. Important events, like her acceptance of Clare's proposal, always take place on the move. These journeys permit Hardy to weave both ancient histories and recent agricultural changes into the text, and enable him to remind us of the key incidents in Tess's life.

Cross-references

As has already been noted, the book has a structure built of coincidences, repetitions, omens and **foreshadowings**, each reliant on the others for support. Overall, we are encouraged to read Tess as doomed. But these links between past and present also provide the reader with a sense of unity, create quite subtle **ironies**, and help build a narrative that entraps the reader.

There are many repeated incidents which take place under altered circumstances. We see Tess at work in the harvest field, the dairy, the rick yard and the open fields. The differences in her experience are highlighted by season, location and employment. Tess is dressed by her mother, then by Marian and Izz, and on both occasions she runs into Alec. Similarly, Tess is dressed up in jewels by Angel, then in finery by Alec. With Hardy's pessimistic tone, these and similar coincidences help generate a pervasive atmosphere of fatalism.

Omens and foreshadowing

Omens include more obvious examples such as the D'Urberville coach and the crowing of the cock on Tess and Angel's wedding day, but also the killing of the Durbeyfields' horse and the way Tess is marked from the outset by a red ribbon. Episodes and characters are carefully woven into a complex pattern and as part of this many events are explicitly prefigured. Alec's murder, for example, is foreshadowed on several occasions, especially when Tess sees herself as a murderess at the end of Chapter 4, and when she strikes him with her gauntlet in Chapter 47.

A05 KEY INTERPRETATION

For an analysis of the ways in which repetition helps to create meaning in *Tess*, read J. Hillis Miller's chapter 'Tess of the D'Urbervilles: Repetition as Immanent Design' in his *Fiction and Repetition: Seven English Novels* (Basil Blackwell, 1982).

There are also more subtle or complex images that work more cumulatively. For example, there is a thread that runs through the text which links Tess's story to the story of Adam and Eve, and makes the outcome of the novel almost inevitable. Also, on several occasions, ancient sites and ancient histories, mingled with folklore and legend, help to make Tess's fate seem inescapable. The numerous tracks Tess travels, the boundaries and borders she crosses, suggest not only her own slow movement along life's path, but also the gradual accumulation of generations of human experience and custom. Those customs stand in stark contrast to the alien and arbitrary railways on which the rural economy depends.

Study focus: The omniscient narrator

The third person, omniscient narrator is an important aspect of *Tess*. The narrator can zoom in and out of the story or skip over large periods of time in order to maintain our interest in Tess's story. Think about what the narrator leaves out, such as Tess's decision to turn to Alec and any representation of her life with him, and consider why Hardy might have made such narratorial choices.

Revision task 9: The role of fate **A02**

Make notes on the ways in which the novel focuses on the influence of fate on ordinary people's lives. You should consider:

- The way in which Tess herself always seems to be trapped by circumstances, despite her beauty and wit
- The other characters, Tess's mother, for example: Is Joan Durbeyfield just as trapped by fate as her daughter?

LANGUAGE

Points of view

When you study the style and language of *Tess* you find that the vocabulary, sentence structure, diction, even the tone, all vary considerably, and this is quite deliberate on Hardy's part. Characters are in part constructed through the way they speak, and when we see something from their **point of view** we catch an echo of their language in the narrative. There are also several letters, providing further variation of style. There is a clear shift between the spoken and the written word when Tess writes to Clare, because to write at all she has to rely on her Sixth Standard education.

Key quotation: Tess's letters   A01

Tess's letters to Angel become more and more desperate in tone as her situation becomes increasingly difficult. Her letter in Chapter 48 ends with 'Come to me – come to me, and save me from what threatens me! – Your faithful, heartbroken Tess' (p. 337).

For the first time in her letters Tess resorts to imperatives here, pleading with Angel to return. Previously she had sought to question and persuade but by the end of this letter she has demonstrated both her enduring love for her correspondent and her sense of injustice in the way he has treated her.

Progress booster: Author or narrator?   A02

It is often difficult to decide through whose eyes a particular scene is being presented, and the reader must consider this very carefully because *Tess of the D'Urbervilles* is not presented from a single point of view. Hardy predominantly uses an **omniscient narrator**, who gives us extra information that the characters do not have access to and who adds speculative asides, such as that at the end of Chapter 37.

The author should not normally be assumed to be the narrator, but sometimes Hardy does seem to intervene. For example, the commentary on the representation of rural people in Chapter 18 overlaps with Hardy's own essay on 'The Dorsetshire Labourer' in *Longman's Magazine* (1883). Hardy also often implies that he is telling a familiar local tale, thereby creating the illusion that the story exists quite independently of its author – for example in Chapter 2. Similarly, he implies that his readers will already know some of the places where the story takes place, such as the house where Tess and Angel stay in Chapter 34. In Chapter 14 he even implies that Tess is a real person.

Consider what effects Hardy creates by suggesting to his readers that he is drawing on real places and stories.

KEY CONTEXT   A03

Dorset County Museum has a gallery on Thomas Hardy. You can visit Thomas Hardy's cottage, in the care of the National Trust, at Higher Bockhampton, Dorset.

Seeing through the characters' eyes

Hardy's detailed descriptions are often seen through the eyes of the main characters, though are presented in the third person. For instance, in Chapter 27 Tess is portrayed as she is seen by Angel, which sets the scene for his first proposal. In Chapter 58 Angel's and Tess's descriptions of Stonehenge add to the strangeness of the landscape. This technique is used to create a sense of involvement, especially with Tess. We know how Tess feels about her Marlott home because we see the cottage through her eyes in Chapter 3, and this helps us to understand something of her relationship with her family and her essential homelessness. Her return home in Chapter 50 similarly provides us with a particularly clear sense of how she sees the world around her; it is indicative of the emotional strain which she is under and allows us to know a little of what she feels about her history to date.

Creating distance

A similar technique is used to opposite effect where the narrative itself is relayed indirectly by secondary or minor characters, as in Chapter 56 when Mrs Brooks finds Alec's body, and Chapter 58 when Tess and Angel are found asleep by the caretaker. This creates a sense of detachment from the feelings of the major characters, while at the same time involving the reader in the events themselves, which are presented to us as if they were being reported in a newspaper or during a trial. The minor characters are not directly involved with what they see and therefore help create a dispassionate yet precise picture of what has happened.

Style

Hardy's style has been characterised as picturesque and occasionally patronising. His diction can be very complex. For example, when describing how Joan Durbeyfield feels when she goes to fetch her husband at Rolliver's, he writes: 'Troubles and other realities took on themselves a metaphysical impalpability, sinking to minor cerebral phenomena for quiet contemplation, in place of standing as pressing concretions which chafe body and soul.' (Chapter 3, p. 23) This use of quasi-scientific, philosophical language sets a considerable distance between a well-educated narrator and their subject. The tone makes us feel as if Joan is being patronised.

Hardy was certainly worried about his writing – he sought to improve it by reading Defoe, Fielding, Addison, Scott and *The Times*. But many passages that seem to be excessively complex create a sense of immediacy, a feeling of almost being drawn into the scene so that the reader sees it as the narrator does. Hardy therefore uses unusual, long words and complex or convoluted sentences with lots of subclauses to create a heightened and more intense vision than could otherwise be achieved. Often this is meant to make us see something ordinary in a new light – a process known as **defamiliarisation**. For example, when Prince's blood is described as 'assuming the iridescence of coagulation' with 'a million prismatic hues reflected from it' (Chapter 4, p. 33), we see the pool of blood in a new way.

A05 **KEY INTERPRETATION**

For more on Hardy's language and style, refer to Ralph W. V. Elliott's detailed study *Thomas Hardy's English* (Basil Blackwell, 1986).

Study focus: A new style

Hardy experimented with language. He was both an observer of and a participant in the changes, issues and people he was writing about, and neither the language of the educated nor the **dialect** of the common people could take account of the experience of modernity that he was hoping to capture. What Hardy was searching for was a new language, a new style, which could carry both precision of observation and intensity of involvement. Hardy was therefore particularly careful in his choice of words. He was a poet as well as a novelist, and you should bear in mind that he kept revising the text, sometimes merely adding or changing a word, right up to 1912.

Dialects and education

Hardy was able to use archaic language like 'Verily' (Chapter 12, p. 75), classical references and foreign words, and chose to attempt a very 'literary' style, because he could expect a highly educated audience for his work. It is also interesting to see how he used this kind of language in such a way as to reflect Angel's character and class. Hardy is able to hint at Angel's increasing influence over Tess when her own speech begins to shift towards a more elevated style reminiscent of the educated tones of the Clare family. This is noticed by Alec, who similarly adopts some of Angel's more religious turns of phrase (in Phase the Sixth: The Convert), in sharp and often direct contrast to his more usual urban slang. As Angel builds on Tess's schooling, while her family and the other working women use the dialect, she continues to speak the dialect at home, and we get a very clear picture of the way in which Tess lives in two worlds.

Study focus: Cinematic juxtaposition

At his best, Hardy can create quite sinister effects through the odd **juxtaposition** of familiar words, such as the 'stagnant obscurity' (Chapter 45, p. 313) of the atmosphere as Tess approaches Flintcomb-Ash. His use of the present tense provides a direct experience of the landscapes he is describing.

You should look out for carefully worked and **ironical** similes in *Tess*, and what might be called Hardy's film-like technique. Tim Dolin has called Hardy a 'cinematic novelist' in the *Blackwell Companion to Hardy*. Consider what this might mean for Hardy's language as well as his narratorial perspective.

Rhythms of language

Hardy uses rhythm to stress the monotony in his characters' lives, or to give a feeling of having no choice, of fatalism. His writing is often heavily punctuated, 'as if to give pause while that word was driven well home to the reader's heart' (Chapter 12, p. 79). He generally gives a quite **naturalistic** rendering to speech, but at times he creates a feeling of intensity through the sense that what they say is measured as if by a beat, especially in dialect, and when people are dealing with stressful situations he tends to use quite **melodramatic** diction. In other words, the question of prose is not as much about having a 'good' style, but about whether or not that style works for the author.

Imagery and symbolism

Visual imagery

Many, or even most, of the symbols that we come across in the novel are in fact omens, but Hardy's narrative often gives the impression of something seen rather than felt. Hardy is an acute observer. Because of his sensitivity to the visual, Hardy often uses graphic effects, such as slogans writ large in red paint, through which he sets up clear moral boundaries, but he equally draws on the subtlest of signs, such as little marks of wear and tear on buildings or furniture which indicate the passage of time at the human level.

Hardy's sensory world

It is worth noting Hardy's use of all of the senses, sometimes interwoven to give an effect of **synaesthesia**. For example, when Tess is listening to Angel play his harp, 'The floating pollen seemed to be his notes made visible' (Chapter 19, p. 123). The aural shades into the visual in this unusual image. In *Tess* the senses can be misled, by the fog in The Chase for example, or by the haze of hay dust at the Chaseborough dance. But sensory experience can also provide exquisite pleasure, such as the 'exaltation' (p. 123) Tess feels when listening to Angel's music.

A02

Progress booster: The colour red

Note how Tess is closely associated with one of the most pervasive images in the text: the colour red. Tess, in a sense, becomes bloodstained. At the opening of the novel she stands out among the other girls because she is wearing a red ribbon against the white background of her dress. When Angel Clare first sees her, he sees that red ribbon. Soon after this she is bathed in Prince's blood and thereafter becomes surrounded by red; even the D'Urberville home is built of red brick. That red is also contained within her, though, as we see when our attention is drawn to the redness of her snake-like mouth. Alec describes her lips as the bright red of holly berries. Think carefully about how Hardy's use of red symbolism shifts as the novel progresses.

Light and darkness

At first, when she dances at the 'club-walking' (Chapter 2, p. 13), Tess is not only mostly white she is also sun-blessed, and this imagery works alongside her redness until sun and blood come together in Phase the Seventh. The sun shines sweetly on Tess while she is still a girl, and continues to do so while she works at the dairy. The summer suns bring fertility and bounty to Talbothays, which is where Tess ripens into full womanhood and where she is happiest.

But the sun does not always shine. Tess and Angel court during the misty, cold, watery hours before dawn, and at these times Tess is spiritually elevated for Clare: she is 'a visionary essence of woman' (Chapter 20, p. 130), only becoming the physical dairymaid that she really is when the sun rises. When Tess finally agrees to marry Angel their lives are held in the balance at the equinox. They finally wed in the middle of winter, close to the longest night. The sun deserts and finally betrays Tess. It becomes a force that stains or marks her, like her red ribbon and the blood of the horse: 'The sun was so low on that short last afternoon of the year that it shone in through a small opening and formed a golden staff which stretched across to her skirt, where it made a spot like a paint-mark set upon her' (Chapter 34, p. 217). The final curtain falls on her as she sleeps in a bed hung about by crimson drapes, revealed by a 'shaft of dazzling sunlight' (Chapter 57, p. 388).

PROGRESS CHECK

Section One: Check your understanding

These tasks will help you to evaluate your knowledge and skills level in this particular area.

1. List three ways in which we might define *Tess* as belonging to the tragedy genre.

2. Make a list of the ways in which this novel lends itself to adaptation for the screen.

3. The narrator in *Tess of the D'Urbervilles* has a patronising attitude towards the protagonist of the novel. Write a paragraph agreeing or disagreeing with this assertion.

4. Make a list of three moments when the narrator deliberately obscures our perspective or withholds information from us. Briefly note why these shifts in perspective occur.

5. Choose three moments when we see the symbolic significance of the colour red, and briefly explain it.

6. List five words that you find obscure or archaic. Give a dictionary definition for each.

7. Compare Angel's speech with Tess's speech when she first arrives at the dairy. Then choose a moment of dialogue between the two characters later on in the novel. What shifts in language use do you find?

8. Make a list of three non-visual symbols in the novel. Do they give different effects in contrast to Hardy's visual imagery?

9. Identify three moments in which dialect is used by one of the minor characters. What does it reveal about the character or the context?

10. Identify three significant words or images that recur in the novel, and briefly describe how their meaning alters according to the context.

PROGRESS BOOSTER   A01

For each Section Two task, read the question carefully, select the key areas you need to address, and plan an essay of six to seven points. Write a first draft, giving yourself an hour to do so. Make sure you include supporting evidence for each point, including quotations.

Section Two: Working towards the exam

Choose one of the following three tasks which require longer, more developed answers.

1. 'In a tragic novel, the protagonist must be flawed in order for their tragedy to be believable.' Do you agree?

2. How does Hardy use both time and space to structure his novel?

3. 'Like many Victorian novelists, Hardy is a realist even when he seems to question the possibilites of realism.' Consider *Tess of the D'Urbervilles* in the light of this statement.

Progress check					
(rate your understanding on a level of 1 – low, to 5 – high)	1	2	3	4	5
How Hardy structures the narrative					
How point of view contributes to characterisation					
How an individual text can modify our understanding of a genre					
The dramatic effect of juxtaposition and mirroring					
The use of vocabulary and imagery for poetic effect within a prose narrative					

CONTEXTS

Historical context

Hardy centres *Tess* in and around Dorset, an agricultural region which, by the time that Hardy was writing, had already undergone considerable economic and social change. There was no longer a 'peasantry', but a society structured by class relations and social mobility. The rural economy was now dependent upon urban markets – Dorset, which was a pastoral county, ultimately did very well out of this – and by the 1890s had been through a long-term depression brought about by shifts in the global economy.

Rural poverty

As a result of this depression, employment had declined drastically and wages had fallen, especially in the south and east of England where arable farming predominated. Gross output fell even in Dorset, despite its specialisation in dairy production, and some tenant farmers in Dorset refused to bind themselves to anything longer than a one-year lease. Thousands had left the countryside in search of work, and a series of education acts passed from the 1870s onwards added to the process of depopulation. There were 18,000 agricultural labourers in Dorset in 1871 and only 12,500 by 1891. The Dorset agricultural labourer lived, generally, in appalling conditions, in fact some of the worst in the country, while class relations were among the most embittered of the time.

A shifting pattern of rural life

Late nineteenth-century rural society was characterised by mobility, insecurity and separation, just like its urban counterpart. We can see this in Tess's constant journeying and movement from farm to farm, but also in the journeys of more minor characters like Marian and Izz, or the way in which the Durbeyfields are thrown out of their home as soon as the last male tenant dies, because they are morally inferior. The agricultural revolution had taken place by the time that Hardy was writing – the railway came to Dorchester when Hardy was seven. What he describes, therefore, is an ongoing, continuous process of change in the countryside, not a static and idealised rural world. Hardy's Wessex is a **pastoral** environment destroyed by new, invasive technologies.

AO3 **KEY CONTEXT**

See Herbert F. Tucker, ed., *A New Companion to Victorian Literature and Culture* (Blackwell, 2014), for a good working introduction to the period. 'Part One: History in Focus' provides four chapters focusing on 1832, 1851, 1870 and 1897, each one providing a snapshot of what life was like in that moment of the Victorian period.

AO5 **KEY INTERPRETATION**

For more on the history of rural England at the time that Hardy was writing, see Alun Howkins, *Reshaping Rural England: A Social History 1850–1925* (HarperCollins, 1991). Social historians are interested in the daily lives of the mass of people at the lower end of the social scale, rather than the small group of elites who have often shaped history.

Study focus: Social relations **AO3**

Hardy was sensitive to the workings of the rural economy and to its actual, everyday social relations. He was not always accurate in terms of detail (a woman would not have worked on a threshing machine in the late 1880s as Tess does); what concerned him was the economic context of that work and the impact of the wider social and moral concerns of his period on people like the Durbeyfields. Consider how the novel shows us that rural life is different for Tess's generation in contrast to her parents' generation.

Settings

The settings in a novel ordinarily provide background, atmosphere and interest; they add a degree of authenticity, and in Hardy's novels can be extremely detailed. In other words they provide the novel with a degree of **verisimilitude** and **realism**. Hardy specialises in a very careful handling of scenery and season, so that time and place reinforce mood. Every detail of the hour, season or landscape echoes a shift in sensibility.

Most of Hardy's settings in *Tess of the D'Urbervilles* underline Tess's development and current condition or well-being. For example, you can contrast her arrival in the valley of the Great Dairies in Chapter 16 with her journey to Flintcomb-Ash in Chapter 42. It is therefore vital that the settings in *Tess* are appreciated in order that the themes of the novel can be understood.

When Hardy assumes that places are unknown to his readers, he goes on to describe them as if writing a travel guide. He often initially sketches a landscape from a height and at a distance and then closes in. One of the best examples of this approach is to be found at the beginning of Chapter 14. Here, Hardy provides a long description of the August harvest at Marlott and, after initially making her an anonymous figure in the landscape, gradually moves, or even zooms, in to focus on Tess as she works among the binders. This particular example in fact sets up a conflict for us. Tess is the absolute focus of attention here; we cannot keep our eyes off her because she is exceptional. Yet she is supposed to be an ordinary field-woman and 'part and parcel of outdoor nature, and … not merely an object set down therein' (Chapter 14, p. 88).

Key quotation: Stonehenge

When Tess and Angel reach Stonehenge at the end of their attempt to escape, Tess says, 'One of my mother's people was a shepherd hereabouts, now I think of it. And you used to say at Talbothays that I was a heathen. So now I am at home.' (Chapter 58, p. 393)

Although Tess spends much of her time at her childhood home in Marlott, it is abruptly taken away from her family on her father's death. By the end of the novel the concept of home is represented as a space of sacrifice. Tess knows that her life will soon be over and since reuniting with Angel the outside world holds little meaning for her.

Literary context

Hardy's literary antecedents include the Romantics, **realists** like George Eliot and the 'rural' authors of his day. What is interesting about Hardy, however, is that he seems to move beyond many of his forebears. For instance, Hardy is critical of the Romantics' view of nature: 'Some people would like to know whence the poet whose philosophy is in these days deemed as profound … gets his authority for speaking of "Nature's holy plan"' (Chapter 3, p. 24). And while, in a way, he returns to their vision of nature, he also sets out to place it within a modern context and undermine their conception of Providence in nature.

The rural context

Books about the countryside proliferated at the end of the century. The desire to read about rural life came about as the countryside became more remote from metropolitan audiences and threatened by competition from abroad, then through depression and depopulation. Authors like Richard Jefferies (1848–87) – *Hodge and His Masters* (1880) and *The Toilers of the Field* (1881), and *The Dewy Morn* (1884) – provided a catalogue of apparently genuine peasants for their readers to enjoy in prose, fiction and verse, while the Baedeker guides of the time documented the details of rural life for the growing tourist industry.

Hardy can be just as silent as any other country author about the horrors of rural life, and frequently slips into the stereotypical portrayal of 'Hodge' (an archetypal working-class labourer) that he criticised in 'The Dorsetshire Labourer'. He describes panoramic views of Wessex that would have done Baedeker proud and captures them for the armchair tourist who wants to preserve a vanishing, primitive way of life.

Tess, however, is not a flat caricature of a seduced peasant girl, but a complex figure who cannot be categorised. She is certainly put on display, and at times she seems to be a tourist attraction who just catches the roving eye, but Tess is also viewed from all possible angles

A03 **KEY CONTEXT**

The term Romanticism covers a range of tendencies in literature, art and culture that emerged at the end of the eighteenth century and dominated the early years of the nineteenth century. It generally involved a movement away from the sceptical, rational and formal culture of the eighteenth century and aimed to liberate the creative imagination.

Revision task 10: Character and landscape **A02**

Consider the landscape through which Tess passes and in which she works. How does it reflect:

● Tess's social and moral standing?
● Tess's inner life and emotions?

Comparative texts

Emily Brontë, *Wuthering Heights* (1847)

Brontë's novel shares a rural setting with Hardy's work, although *Wuthering Heights* is set in the North of England while *Tess of the D'Urbervilles* takes Hardy's southern home county as its setting. In both works the rural setting is also aligned with superstition, and the rural **dialect** of the uneducated characters, such as the servant Joseph, contrasts with the vocabulary of the more refined Edgar Linton. Both novels might be described as **tragedies**, both plots work against their protagonists and send them to their deaths. However, neither Cathy nor Heathcliff (the central characters in *Wuthering Heights*) are as subject to the operations of fate as Tess is. Both are complex characters whose flaws and inconsistencies help to bring about their demise. Consider the role of the framing narrative in *Wuthering Heights* and whether it distances us from the action, despite the first-person giving us insight into several characters.

George Eliot, *The Mill on the Floss* (1860)

KEY CONNECTION   **A04**

Khaled Hosseini's novel *A Thousand Splendid Suns* (2008) provides many points of comparison with *Tess of the D'Urbervilles* in relation to the theme of women in society. Set in Afghanistan, from the mid-twentieth century to the present day, its immediate context is very different, but it also deals with illegitimacy and the struggle for female independence in a male-dominated society.

Maggie Tulliver, the central character in *The Mill on the Floss,* shares some affinities with Tess Durbeyfield. Both are ambitious young women whose paths in life are hampered by the gender conventions of their time. Hardy and Eliot are keen to show their readers the inner complexities of their female protagonists – both are highly intelligent women denied the chance of a formal education. One of the central events in Maggie's life is her near-elopement with the man she loves, Stephen Guest, who is engaged to another woman. However, Maggie turns back at the crucial moment, whereas Hardy's narrative takes all agency away from Tess and makes her a passive victim of Alec. We might argue that both Hardy and Eliot place their protagonists at the apex of conflicts between tradition and change, and between free will and determinism.

Charlotte Brontë, *Jane Eyre* (1847)

Brontë's novel, like Hardy's, takes an eponymous young woman as its protagonist. But Tess and Jane come from different class backgrounds and this has a significant impact on the extent of education they receive and on their final fates. Jane's story ends with marriage and children; Tess's story ends with death. We might also consider the role of religious belief in both novels. Both Hardy and Brontë provide individuals whose religious faith is zealous, self-destructive, or destructive of the happiness of others. Think of Helen Burns, Jane's childhood friend, or compare St John River's self-sacrificing determination with that of Angel's father or even of Alec.

Seamus Heaney, 'Punishment' (from *North*, published 1975)

Heaney's poems asks us to consider the historical punishment of a woman he calls 'Little adulteress'. The speaker of the poem imagines the woman's body naked, hanged, drowned, blindfold, shaven-headed, stripped by a cruel society of her dignity and individuality. The speaker also sees themselves as complicit in the revenge carried out against the fallen woman. Hardy, like Heaney, attempts to make his readers consider the inequities in society's treatment of illegitimate sexuality in women and men.

Study focus: Love poetry comparisons   **A04**

Hardy's own 'The Ruined Maid' provides an obvious connection with *Tess,* although the speaker is much more blasé about her 'ruin' than Tess's. Hardy refuses to condemn the fallen women in either of the texts. Keats's 'La Belle Dame sans Merci' develops chivalric imagery alongside an idea of love as an enchantment that ultimately leads to desolation. Consider 'To His Coy Mistress' by John Donne in the light of Alec's attempts to seduce Tess and, indeed, Angel's attempts to persuade Tess to marry him.

CRITICAL INTERPRETATIONS

Reception and early critical reviews

Tess of the D'Urbervilles: A Pure Woman was not well received by critics when it was first published. The *Quarterly Review* declared that the subtitle put 'a strain upon the English language'. *The Independent* said that the novel was 'a pretty kettle of fish for pure people to eat' and that it threatened 'the moral fibre of young readers'. *Punch, or the London Charivari* produced a satire of the novel in 1892. Called 'Bo and the Blacksheep', this was a one-page pastiche of the novel in which Bonduca, or Bo Peep, 'had a flexuous and finely-drawn figure not unreminiscent of many a vanished night and dame'.

Courting controversy

The contemporary critics largely focused on the question of Hardy's morality. A few preferred to concentrate on the issue of Hardy's style or the plausibility of the story, but most critics attacked Hardy as a libertine because of the novel's subject matter and because he had chosen to describe Tess as 'pure' in the subtitle. An unmarried woman, who had lost her virginity, had an illegitimate child and become entangled in an ultimately adulterous relationship leading to murder could not be 'pure' in the view of most readers.

Hardy thought that the critics were reading his novel too literally and argued, 'I still maintain that her innate purity remained intact to the very last; though I frankly own that a certain outward purity left her on her last fall. I regarded her then as being in the hands of circumstances, not morally responsible, a mere corpse drifting with the current.'

Later criticism

Despite the highly controversial start to the novel's career, *Tess* rapidly became, and still is, a very popular novel. What becomes particularly clear when we look at the various readings of *Tess*, is that both the novel and its protagonist have been interpreted in very different ways. Today it is Angel who is more likely to be attacked than Tess herself. Many critics have in fact found it hard to believe in the double standard to which Tess falls victim. They suggest that Hardy might be able to convince us that Angel is a hypocrite, but wonder that Angel cannot see any resemblance at all between his past and Tess's.

A novelist of country life

Hardy languished for many years in partial obscurity as a fairly minor writer. Seen as a self-taught peasant, he was predominantly thought of as a quaint local author who catalogued the decay of a vanishing, more rural way of life, who was good at dialect and faintly hostile to new industrial technologies. Critics therefore focused on his detailed accounts of folklore and village or local custom. He was seen as a good regional novelist who wrote about and came from the peasantry. Wessex is still widely sold to tourists via Hardy's writing.

If we accept this approach, *Tess* might be seen as the culmination of Hardy's best work about the countryside. Tess's **tragedy** lies in her anomalous social position, caused by her D'Urberville blood, a position which represents the tragedy of rural England in which the old aristocracy gives way to a new urban elite, who do not understand or care for the land and its people.

A03 KEY CONTEXT

Punch's satire 'Mr. Punch's Agricultural Novel. Bo and the Blacksheep. A story of *the Sex*' by 'Thomas of Wessex' was published on 7 May 1892. It concludes: 'And, from the calm nonchalance of a Wessex hamlet, another novel was launched into a world of reviews, where the multitude of readers is not as to their external displacements, but as to their subjective experiences.'

A03 KEY CONTEXT

To put *Tess* into the wider context of Victorian literature and its history of criticism, see Francis O'Gorman, ed., *The Victorian Novel* (Blackwell, 2002).

Class and modernity

Similarly, *Tess* has frequently been read as being about the fall of the English peasantry, in which case Tess becomes the representative of that peasantry, sent away from the idyllic world of her childhood to become the victim of Alec, son of a successful merchant. Once out of his clutches, she is then subject to Angel, the urban intellectual, and slave to the needs of the threshing machine, which is symbolic of her final and complete degradation as caused by the invasion of everything that is out of sympathy with the rhythms of rural life.

Cultural materialism

A new approach finally emerged when the cultural materialists reappraised Hardy in the 1970s. Cultural materialists are interested in situating texts within their specific historical contexts. They analyse how texts conform to or reject the dominant ideologies of their historical moment. Cultural materialists saw Hardy as a major author, whose chief merit lay in his sympathetic treatment and understanding of the labourer, and as an author who could represent the key issues of the modern age.

Though Hardy was not of the labouring class himself, cultural materialists saw him as a radical author, critical of class relations, as characterised by Tess's subjection to economic need and abuse. These critics also highlighted the importance of historical context by pointing out that the English peasantry were long gone by the time that Hardy was writing. By the 1870s, they argue, the countryside was already structured by social mobility, hence Tess's use of **dialect** with her family – self-employed hagglers – and standard English with her 'betters'. And, they stress, Hardy was well aware of the appalling conditions of rural life in the 1870s; it is clear, for instance, that the Durbeyfields exist only on the barest margins of economic survival.

Many critics have persisted in focusing on Hardy's concept of community despite this, and the text is still widely and simply praised for its accuracy and **verisimilitude** in respect of rural life. But some well-considered arguments have emerged against this reading, which stress that it is not meant to be a representative or **realist** text. The cultural materialist reading of *Tess* as social criticism has not convinced all subsequent critics, but – and this is related to their new approach – many have come to focus to a greater extent on Hardy's philosophy and ideology.

Contemporary approaches

Feminist criticism

Hardy clearly worked hard at defending Tess's purity and the morality of the novel itself, and many critics have now come to realise that in putting Tess, in a sense, on trial, it is 'purity' itself and the right to define it that is in fact tried. If the novel is read in this way, it is possible to see *Tess of the D'Urbervilles* as a feminist text. This is because the society that damns Tess as impure is essentially patriarchal. She is too complex a woman to be understood by a society that classifies women under the headings 'virgin' or 'whore'. It can be argued that Hardy is very much in love with his 'Tessy' and as such cannot condone what happens to her. We may of course then wonder whether he succeeds in handling the issues he raises, but that is a separate question.

Many feminist critics still consider the novel to be misogynistic. They argue that Tess is treated as a spectacle in the novel and is presented to us as an object for display. Tess is looked at in detail, from near and far; we gaze into the depths of her eyes, we see her working as a figure in the landscape, we consider her every 'aspect'. This is partly because she is a woman, they suggest, and feminists argue that women are exhibited as objects for the male gaze within patriarchy, but Hardy's heightened visual approach underlines this process and makes it especially forceful.

Marxist criticism

This approach to literary texts emphasises class struggle. The nineteenth-century German thinker, Karl Marx, argued that the working classes are oppressed and alienated by the wealthy ruling class who control every aspect of their lives. He encouraged the idea that this capitalist class system could ultimately be overthrown.

A Marxist reading of *Tess of the D'Urbervilles* would emphasise the difficulties of life for the rural poor whose labour profits the landowners much more than it does themselves. We might also consider the way in which Hardy himself criticises the systems by which labour is organised in the Victorian period. Families like the D'Urbervilles have been oppressed by the system and it offers them no realistic way out. Jack Durbeyfield falls back on a fantasy of class mobility which damages his family and Tess in particular. Farmer Groby at Flintcomb-Ash is a good example of an employer who cares nothing for those who labour for him and the reader is left in little doubt that the narrator disapproves of this character. Alec D'Urberville is also a contemptible character: he has inherited wealth and does not need to work; instead, his time is spent in questionable pursuits such as his many attempts to seduce Tess.

WORKERS OF ALL LANDS

 A05 KEY INTERPRETATION

For a thought-provoking example of feminist criticism, see Judith Weissman, *Half Savage and Hardy and Free: Women and Rural Radicalism in the Nineteenth-Century Novel* (Wesleyan University Press, 1987).

A04 KEY CONTEXT

Taken from feminist psychoanalytic film theory, 'the male gaze' suggests that women are objectified within patriarchy. It links the subjectivity and subjection of women to the process of representation and the pleasure of looking. Femininity is formed through spectacle, masculinity through the gaze.

KEY INTERPRETATION

Another recent school of criticism relevant to *Tess of the D'Urbervilles* is **ecocriticism**, which looks at how texts respond to and reflect environmental forces. The text is full of references to the natural world and how it interacts with the human world – through the process of rural ritual, which Hardy is sympathetic to, and then industrialisation, of which Hardy is critical.

New historicist criticism

'New historicism' is a term coined by the critic Stephen Greenblatt. This approach suggests that literature should be read in conjunction with other non-literary texts in order to help us understand particular cultural and social contexts.

A key reading that has recently gained currency among a number of new historicist critics is one which reads Hardy's work in the light of Charles Darwin's scientific texts such as *On the Origin of Species* (1859) and *The Descent of Man* (1877). The influence of Darwin's evolutionary theory on Hardy's thought is drawn out in the way in which Tess seems to repeat or is subject to the acts of her ancestors. She is haunted, not only by the D'Urberville coach, but also by the portraits of the D'Urberville women which Angel cannot get out of his mind after Tess's confession, and whom she physically and mentally resembles. She takes on the appearance of a lady when she is dressed in the jewels Angel gives her, her figure is finer than any of the other working women and she, like her father, is often quite conceited.

This Darwinian subtext is said to provide an alternative, **naturalist** voice in the novel which undercuts much of Hardy's defence of Tess as a simple peasant maid who is a victim of her society. She often acts wilfully because of a misplaced sense of pride, and when she remains passive her fate seems to be determined as much by her heredity as her environment.

Psychoanalytic criticism

Sigmund Freud (see portrait, left) is known as the father of psychoanalysis. He developed theories suggesting that human behaviour is determined primarily by our unconscious desires. We only perceive these desires through dreams or slips of the tongue.

A literary critic using a psychoanalyst's approach would look closely at Tess's and Angel's dreams, fantasies and reveries. Of significant interest would be the episode in Chapter 37 when Angel carries Tess to a ruined abbey and places her in a coffin. We could argue that Tess's admission of her lost virginity has caused her symbolic death in Angel's eyes. His inner desires might be to rid himself of his new wife, or at least the version of Tess that has disappointed him. He may also have an inner desire that the symbolic death might allow Tess to be re-born into a state of innocence. It is also significant that during his sleep-walking episode he 'took advantage of the handrail to imprint a kiss upon her lips – lips in the daytime scorned' (Chapter 37, p. 247).

PROGRESS CHECK

Section One: Check your understanding

These tasks will help you to evaluate your knowledge and skills level in this particular area.

1. Make a table demonstrating at least three ways in which wealth and poverty are contrasted in *Tess of the D'Urbervilles*.

2. Make a table contrasting key characteristics of the world of Tess's family with the world of Angel's family.

3. List three forms of technology that play a role in the story of *Tess of the D'Urbervilles*. Include a brief description of the role played by each.

4. Make a list of three reasons why setting is a vital factor in Hardy's work.

5. Make a table listing three or four points of connection between *Tess of the D'Urbervilles* and any other text that you have studied.

6. Write a paragraph outlining the reasons why Hardy's contemporary critics were shocked when *Tess of the D'Urbervilles* was first published.

7. Write a paragraph outlining what you understand by the term 'realism'.

8. List three events that might provide focal points for a feminist reading of the novel. Briefly describe the significance of each for such a reading.

9. List three moments in the text that a cultural materialist critic might highlight, and explain why.

10. What kind of insights might be gained from an ecocritical reading of *Tess of the D'Urbervilles*? Write a paragraph outlining your ideas.

Section Two: Working towards the exam

Choose one of the following three tasks which require longer, more developed answers.

1. Consider the significance of rural life in *Tess of the D'Urbervilles* and in any other novel written in the nineteenth century.

2. Examine the relationship between Tess and Angel using three different critical approaches (e.g. feminist, new historicist, Marxist).

3. 'Hardy's novel emphasises how historical forces operate on individual lives.' Do you agree with this statement?

A01 PROGRESS BOOSTER

For each Section Two task, read the question carefully, select the key areas you need to address, and plan an essay of six to seven points. Write a first draft, giving yourself an hour to do so. Make sure you include supporting evidence for each point, including quotations.

Progress check

(rate your understanding on a level of 1 – low, to 5 – high)	1	2	3	4	5
How some knowledge of context enhances interpretation of the novel					
The different ways the novel can be read, according to critical approaches such as feminist or new historicist					
How comparison with another literary work can deepen understanding of both					
How a reader's interpretation may differ from the author's intended meaning					
How *Tess of the D'Urbervilles* can be read as a historical document					

ASSESSMENT FOCUS

How will you be assessed?

Each particular exam board and exam paper will be slightly different, so make sure you check with your teacher exactly which Assessment Objectives you need to focus on. You are likely to get more marks for Assessment Objectives 1, 2 and 3, if you are studying AQA A or B, but this does not mean you should discount 4 or 5. Bear in mind that if you are doing AS Level, although the weightings are the same, there will be no coursework element.

What do the AOs actually mean?

	Assessment Objective	Meaning?
AO1	Articulate informed, personal and creative responses to literary texts, using associated concepts and terminology, and coherent, accurate written expression.	You write about texts in accurate, clear and precise ways so that what you have to say is clear to the marker. You use literary terms (e.g. **'irony'**) or refer to concepts (e.g. 'the fallen woman') in relevant places. You do not simply repeat what you have read or been told, but express your own ideas based on in-depth knowledge of the text and related issues.
AO2	Analyse ways in which meanings are shaped in literary texts.	You are able to explain in detail how the specific techniques and methods used by Hardy to create the text (e.g. **narrative** voice, **dialogue**, **metaphor**) influence and affect the reader's response.
AO3	Demonstrate understanding of the significance and influence of the contexts in which literary texts are written and received.	You can explain how the text might reflect the social, historical, political or personal backgrounds of Hardy or the time when the novel was written. You also consider how *Tess of the D'Urbervilles* might have been received differently over time.
AO4	Explore connections across literary texts.	You are able to explain links between *Tess of the D'Urbervilles* and other texts, perhaps of a similar genre, or with similar concerns, or viewed from a similar perspective (e.g. feminist).
AO5	Explore literary texts informed by different interpretations.*	You understand how *Tess of the D'Urbervilles* can be viewed in different ways, and are able to write about these debates, forming your own opinion – for example, how one critic might view Tess as a symbol of gender inequality and another might see her as a victim of poverty and shifts in the rural economy.

* AO5 is not assessed by Edexcel in relation to *Tess of the D'Urbervilles*.

What does this mean for your revision?

Whether you are following an AS or A Level course, use the right-hand column above to measure how confidently you can address these objectives. Then focus your revision on those aspects you feel need most attention. Remember, throughout these Notes, the AOs are highlighted, so you can flick through and check them in that way.

Next, use the tables on page 75. These help you understand the differences between a satisfactory and an outstanding response.

Then, use the guidance from page 76 onwards to help you address the key AOs, for example how to shape and plan your writing.

Features of **mid-level** responses: the following examples relate to Tess's role in the novel.

	Features	Examples
AO1	You use critical vocabulary appropriately for most of the time, and your arguments are relevant to the task, ordered sensibly, with clear expression. You show detailed knowledge of the text.	Tess is the **protagonist** of the novel. The story tells her life from the end of her childhood into early adulthood. We get to know Tess through a **third-person narrator**.
AO2	You show straightforward understanding of the writer's methods, such as how form, structure and language shape meanings.	Hardy **creates sympathy** for Tess as a 'pure' woman who has been wronged. He **draws the reader into her life** by describing her hopes, emotions and responses to other characters in great detail. Hardy does not want the reader to judge Tess but to **sympathise** with her tragic circumstances.
AO3	You can write about a range of contextual factors and make some relevant links between these and the task or text.	The **idea of class** is important in the novel, it sets up barriers between Tess and the men who love her. We see how Tess is trapped within her lower-class, rural life.
AO4	You consider straightforward connections between texts and write about them clearly and relevantly to the task.	The injustice of Tess's fate is connected to her role as a woman in Victorian society. Other Victorian texts take issue with inequality between the sexes, for example, Charlotte Perkin Gilman's **'The Yellow Wallpaper'** also demonstrates the relative powerlessness of women in a patriarchal society.
AO5	You tackle the debate in the task in a clear, logical way, showing your understanding of different interpretations.	Some would argue that Tess is at the mercy of her fate and role is a passive one, **but it could equally be said that her movements across Wessex structure the novel,** and that her final violent action in murdering Alec is also a way of taking control of her life.

Features of a **high-level** response: these examples relate to a task on narrative perspectives.

	Features	Examples
AO1	You are perceptive, and assured in your argument in relation to the task. You make fluent, confident use of literary concepts and terminology; and express yourself confidently.	The novel is one in which the **perspective** is that of an **anonymous third person narrator**. Although the narrator is never named it seems clear that they are educated and probably male, particularly when the narration focuses on Tess's face and body to emphasise her beauty. We might align the narrator with Angel and Alec, who both attempt to exert control over Tess's body.
AO2	You explore and analyse key aspects of Hardy's use of form, structure and language and evaluate perceptively how they shape meanings.	The narrative sometimes allows us to see Tess's internal thoughts – such as her discomfort at attempting to see Angel's parents in Chapter 44 – but also moves away from Tess at some of the key moments in the novel, such as the murder of Alec which we see through the landlady's eyes. **The shifting proximity of narrator and protagonist creates a mixture of sympathy and distance for the reader.**
AO3	You show deep, detailed and relevant understanding of how contextual factors link to the text or task.	The **changing nature of agricultural life** in the nineteenth century is highlighted as Tess's family are thrown into crisis when they lose their home and cannot compete with other rural families for scarce accommodation. The reaping and threshing machines that we see bring increased productivity and wealth to farmers and landowners, but the lives of individual workers are not improved.
AO4	You show a detailed and perceptive understanding of issues raised through connections between texts. You have a range of excellent supportive references.	Tragedy, in its classical incarnation in **works by Sophocles**, for example, proceeds from the actions of a great man brought down by a fundamental weakness. However, **Tess is beset by events over which she has little or no control**. Her status as a rural woman of the working classes offers her no means to escape from her tragic fate.
AO5	You are able to use your knowledge of critical debates and the possible perspectives on an issue to write fluently and confidently about how the text might be interpreted.	Hardy stresses that Tess is a 'pure' woman throughout the novel and draws attention to the double standard by which Angel judges his own sexual morality more leniently than Tess's. Some feminist critics have, however, questioned how liberal Hardy's position on female sexuality really is; after all, **Tess is still punished for her perceived contravention of acceptable behaviour for women.**

HOW TO WRITE HIGH-QUALITY RESPONSES

The quality of your writing – how you express your ideas – is vital for getting a higher grade, and **AO1** and **AO2** are specifically about **how** you respond.

Five key areas

The quality of your responses can be broken down into **five** key areas.

1. The structure of your answer/essay

- First, get **straight to the point in your opening paragraph**. Use a sharp, direct first sentence that deals with a key aspect and then follow up with evidence or detailed reference.
- **Put forward an argument or point of view** (you won't **always** be able to challenge or take issue with the essay question, but generally, where you can, you are more likely to write in an interesting way).
- **Signpost your ideas** with connectives and references which help the essay flow. Aim to present an overall argument or conceptual response to the task, not a series of unconnected points.
- **Don't repeat points already made**, not even in the conclusion, unless you have something new to add.

Aiming high: Effective opening paragraphs

Let's imagine you have been asked about the role of **narrators** in tragedies. Here's an example of a successful opening paragraph:

> Early in the novel, in Chapter 2, the narrator singles out Tess from the group of girls she dances with, just as Angel does. For the narrator she is special and uniquely beautiful but we are also told that to 'almost everybody she was a fine and picturesque country girl, and no more'. The narrator enables us to see that the tragedy of this novel is not just about an individual but also about the way in which any woman of Tess's class could suffer a similarly tragic fate in world in which women were not valued equally with men. How then do we deal with the narrator's relationship to Tess? Does the narrator serve to make Tess's tragedy seem inevitable in her historical context, or does the narratorial voice hint at the possibility of happiness for the heroine?

Immediately identifies a particular moment as a means of opening up the debate

Sets up some interesting ideas that will be tackled in subsequent paragraphs

2. Use of titles, names, etc.

This is a simple, but important, tip to stay on the right side of the examiners.

- Make sure that you spell correctly the titles of the texts, chapters, authors and so on. Present them correctly too, with inverted commas and capitals as appropriate. For example, In 'Tess of the D'Urbervilles'....
- Use the **full title**, unless there is a good reason not to (e.g. it's very long).
- Use the term 'text' rather than 'book' or 'story'. If you use the word 'story', the examiner may think you mean the plot/action rather than the 'text' as a whole.

3. Effective quotations

Do not 'bolt on' quotations to the points you make. You will get some marks for including them, but examiners will not find your writing very fluent.

The best quotations are:

- Relevant and not too long (you are going to have to memorise them, so that will help you select shorter ones!)
- Integrated into your argument/sentence
- Linked to effect and implications

Aiming high: Effective use of quotations

Here is an example of an effective use of a quotation about social class in the novel:

short, relevant quotation, embedded in sentence

When one of Angel's brothers exclaims 'Dancing in public with a troop of country hoydens – suppose we should be seen!', it is more than just a refusal to dance with Tess and the club-walkers. It also sets up the fundamental class divide between Angel and Tess that cannot be ignored.

explicit meaning

inferred meaning

Remember – quotations can be one or two single words or phrases embedded in a sentence to build a picture or explanation, or they can be longer ones that are explored and picked apart.

4. Techniques and terminology

By all means mention literary terms, techniques, conventions, critical theories or people (for example, 'paradox', 'archetype', 'feminism' or 'Freud') **but** make sure that you:

- Understand what they mean or who they are
- Are able to link them to what you're saying
- Spell them correctly

5. General writing skills

Try to write in a way that sounds professional and uses standard English. This does not mean that your writing will lack personality – just that it will be authoritative.

- Avoid colloquial or everyday expressions such as 'got', 'alright', 'ok' and so on.
- Use terms such as 'convey', 'suggest', 'imply', 'infer' to explain the writer's methods.
- Refer to 'we' when discussing the audience/reader.
- Avoid assertions and generalisations; don't just state a general point of view (e.g. 'Angel is a flawed male character and judges Tess too harshly'), but analyse closely with clear evidence and textual detail.

Note the professional approach here in the choice of vocabulary and awareness of the effect on the reader:

When Tess and Angel reach their honeymoon destination in Chapter 3 we might anticipate that this moment will be a fulfilment of Tess and Angel's love but Hardy shows the marriage is doomed through the decrepit setting and through devices like the cock's crow. These give the prose an almost Gothic sense of unfolding tragedy.

EXAMINER'S TIP

Something examiners often comment on is that students can confuse 'narrator' and 'author'. Remember that Hardy is not the narrator; the narrator is an anonymous presence who guides our reading but who is distinct from the author.

QUESTIONS WITH STATEMENTS, QUOTATIONS OR VIEWPOINTS

One type of question you may come across is one that includes a statement, quotation or viewpoint from another reader. You are likely to be asked this about *Tess of the D'Urbervilles* – or about *Tess of the D'Urbervilles* and another text you have studied.

These questions ask you to respond to, or argue for/against, a specific **point of view** or critical interpretation. This is likely to be in relation to the genre of tragedy.

For *Tess of the D'Urbervilles* a typical question would be:

> **'Tragedies do not allow their protagonists any choice; the tragic fate is an inescapable one.' To what extent do you agree with this view in relation to the two texts you have studied, bearing in mind the ways the writers have constructed their texts?'**

The key thing to remember is that you are being asked to **respond to a particular perspective or critical view** of the text – in other words, to come up with **your own** 'take' on the idea or viewpoint in the task.

Key skills required

The table below provides help and advice on answering the question above.

Skill	Means?	How do I achieve this?
To focus on the specific aspect, by exploring Hardy's authorial methods	You must show your understanding of tragedy as a genre which writers use, first tackling whether tragedies do trap their protagonists in inescapable fates and secondly commenting on the degree to which choice is denied the protagonist in this novel.	You will need to deal with the issue generally, either in an opening paragraph or in several paragraphs, but also make sure you keep on coming back to the issue throughout the essay, rather than diverting into other areas which you have not been asked about.
To consider different interpretations	There will be more than one way of looking at the given question. For example, critics might be divided about the extent to which Tess has any choice over her own fate.	Show you have considered these different interpretations in your answer. For example, a student might write: *Tess tells her brother that theirs is a 'blighted' world and sets up a sense of cruel fatality, but there are some moments in which Tess seems hopeful of her future, such as when she sets out on her journey to Talbothays.*
To write with a clear, personal voice	Your own 'take' on the question is made obvious to the examiner. You are not just repeating other people's ideas, but offering what **you** think.	Although you may mention different perspectives on the task, you settle on your own view. Use language that shows careful, but confident, consideration. For example: *Although it has been said that Tess is objectified by the male characters and the narrator, I feel that she is much more than a passive object. In fact, it is Tess's sense of pride that provides the impetus for much of the novel's structure.*
To construct a coherent argument	The examiner or marker can follow your train of thought so that your own viewpoint is clear to him or her.	Write in clear paragraphs that deal logically with different aspects of the question. Support what you say with well-selected and relevant evidence. Use a range of connectives to help 'signpost' your argument. For example: *We might say that Tess loves Angel with a blind and idealising passion. However, her letter to her absent husband does call him to account for his behaviour. Moreover, it is through the writing of these letters that we most distinctly hear Tess's voice independent of the filtering of a male narrator.*

Answering a 'viewpoint' question

Let us look at another question:

> **'The central factor in all tragedies is the suffering and ultimate death of the protagonist.'**
>
> **To what extent do you agree with this view in relation to the two texts you have studied, bearing in mind the ways the writers have constructed their texts?**

Stage 1: Decode the question

Underline/highlight the **key words**, and make sure you understand what the statement, quotation or viewpoint is saying. In this case:

'To what extent do you agree …' means: *Do you wholly agree with this statement or are there aspects of it that you would dispute?*

'The central factor in all tragedies …' means: *Tragedies are organised or built around a core idea (in this case 'suffering' and 'death')*

'protagonist' means: *leading character in the story*

'ultimate death' means: *the tragedy ends with the death of the central character*

So you are being asked whether you agree/disagree with *the idea that every tragedy is dependent upon the suffering and death of its protagonist.*

Stage 2: Decide what your viewpoint is

Examiners have stated that they tend to reward a strong view which is clearly put. Disagreeing strongly can lead to higher marks, provided you have **genuine evidence** to support your point of view. However, don't disagree just for the sake of it.

Stage 3: Decide how to structure your answer

Pick out the key points you wish to make, and decide on the order that you will present them in. Keep this basic plan to hand while you write your response.

Stage 4: Write your response

Begin by expanding on the aspect or topic mentioned in the task title. In this way, you can set up the key ideas you will explore. For example:

> *Many Shakespearean tragedies display the suffering of their central characters caused by a sense of loss or bereavement, as in 'King Lear' or 'Hamlet'. These tragic protagonists seem to hasten their own death by making bad choices in their private and political lives. In 'Tess of the D'Urbervilles', however, the female protagonist's choices are limited by her class and her gender. Her tragedy does not come about because of her elevated or special status; the fact that she is an ordinary young woman makes us sympathise with her suffering all the more.*

Then in the remaining paragraphs proceed to set out the different arguments or perspectives, including your own.

In the final paragraph, end with a clear statement of your viewpoint, but do not list or go over the points you have made. End succinctly and concisely.

Then, proceed to dealing with the second text in a similar way.

> **EXAMINER'S TIP**
>
> You should comment concisely, professionally and thoughtfully and present a range of viewpoints. Try using modal verbs such as 'would', 'could', 'might', 'may' to clarify your own interpretation. For example, *I would argue that to say Angel Clare is in love with Tess does not reveal the whole truth. It might be more accurate to suggest that Angel is in love with an idealised version of Tess.*

COMPARING *TESS OF THE D'URBERVILLES* WITH OTHER TEXTS

EXAMINER'S TIP

Remember that, for the AQA A or B specifications, in order to score highly in your answer you will also need to discuss what the critics say (AO5) and consider relevant cultural or contextual factors (AO3). AO5 is not assessed by Edexcel in relation to *Tess*.

As part of your assessment, you may have to compare *Tess of the D'Urbervilles* with or link it to other texts you have studied. These may be other novels, plays or even poetry. You may also have to link or draw in references from texts written by critics.

Linking or comparison questions might relate to a particular theme or idea, such as 'love'. For example:

> **By exploring the writers' methods, compare ideas about passion in one prose text and one poetry text you have studied.**

Or:

> **Compare the ways in which the writers of your two chosen texts portray women's relationships with men. You must relate your discussion to relevant contextual factors.**

You will need to:

Evaluate the issue or statement and have an **open-minded approach**. The best answers suggest meaning**s** and interpretation**s** (plural):

- For example, in relation to the first question: Do you think that passion can be represented through dialogue, metaphor, or symbolism? Why might a writer draw on any of these devices? And what effects might they seek to achieve? Is one more effective than another at conveying passion in literature?
- What are the different ways in which this question or aspect can be read or viewed?
- What evidence is there in each text for this perspective? How can you present it in a thoughtful, reflective way?
- What are the points of similarity and difference?

Express **original or creative approaches** fluently:

- This isn't about coming up with entirely new ideas, but you need to show that you're actively engaged with thinking about the question, not just reeling off things you have learnt.
- **Synthesise** your ideas – pull ideas and points together to create something fresh.
- This is a linking/comparison response, so ensure that you guide your reader through your ideas logically, clearly and with professional language.

Know *what* to compare/contrast: the writer's methods – **form, structure** and **language** – will **always** be central to your response. Consider:

- The authorial perspective or voice (who is speaking/writing) – standard versus more conventional narration (use of flashback, foreshadowing, or narrative voice which leads to dislocation or difficulty in reading)
- Different characteristic use of language (length of sentences, formal/informal style, dialect, accent, balance of dialogue and narration; difference between prose treatment of an idea and that of a poem)
- Variety of symbols, images, motifs (how they represent concerns of author/time; what they are and how and where they appear; how they link to critical perspectives; their purposes, effects and impact on the narration)
- Shared or differing approaches (to what extent do Hardy and the author(s) of Text 2/3 conform to/challenge/subvert approaches to writing about passion?)

Writing your response

> By exploring the writers' methods, compare ideas about passion in one prose text and one poetry text you have studied.

Introduction to your response

Either discuss quickly what passion is and where you have seen it represented in *Tess of the D'Urbervilles* and two poems you have studied, or start with a particular moment from one of the texts which allows you to launch your exploration. For example, you could use a powerful quotation:

> *'Resolutions, reticences, prudences, fears, fell back like a defeated battalion' when Angel first clasps Tess in his arms. Here passion seems like a struggle against oneself, something which must be battled against but ultimately cannot be controlled. Incidents of passion in 'Tess of the D'Urbervilles' are usually seen as fleeting moments when self-control is lost. However, this loss of self-control can lead to tragic consequences.*

Main body of your response

- **Point 1**: continue your exploration of moments of passion in *Tess of the D'Urbervilles*: What does it suggest about Tess and Angel's relationship? Why might this depiction of their relationship have been controversial? And why was the depiction of sexual desire or passion not the norm in nineteenth-century novels?

- **Point 2**: now cover a new factor or aspect through comparison or contrast of this relationship with another in Text 2 and/or 3. For example, *In Edna St. Vincent Millay's poem 'I, being born a woman and distressed',* sexual passion is similarly seen as a fleeting 'frenzy' which 'cloud[s] the mind'. How is/are the new relationship(s) in Text 2 presented **differently or similarly** by the writer according to language, form, structures used; why was this done in this way?

- **Points 3, 4, 5, etc.**: address a range of other factors and aspects, for example moments of passion in *Tess of the D'Urbervilles* (such as Tess's murder of Alec) **or** in both *Tess of the D'Urbervilles* and the two poems. What different ways do you respond to these (with more empathy, greater criticism, less interest) – and why? For example:

> *We might argue that moments of passion in Tess of the D'Urbervilles inevitably lead to death. When Angel returns to find that Tess has become Alec's mistress in Chapter 55 she speaks 'rapidly' using exclamations and short broken sentences. Her feelings are too intense to be clearly expressed in language. When Tess stabs Alec we hear a repeated 'low note of moaning' and again Tess's conversation with Alec is reported in broken sentences and abrupt exclamations. The final breakdown of control culminating in the passionate stabbing of Alec is foreshadowed by the way in which Tess makes her own lip bleed by the furious clenching of her teeth. Passion is thus a dangerous force and when it is released in Tess its intensity proves fatal.*

Conclusion

- Synthesise elements of what you have said into a succinct final paragraph which leaves the marker with the sense that you have engaged with the task and texts. For example:

> *In 'I, being born a woman, and distressed', sexual passion is likened to a momentary loss of self-control, while in Marvell's 'To His Coy Mistress' sexual passion again seems transient and related to the fleetingness of time. However, in Hardy's 'Tess of the D'Urbervilles', the moment of passion signifies a loss of control which can be dangerous and will have lasting consequences.*

EXAMINER'S TIP

If you are following an AS course, you may have less exam time to write than for the A level – so concise, succinct points with less elaboration than provided here may be needed.

USING CRITICAL INTERPRETATIONS AND PERSPECTIVES

What is a critical interpretation?

The particular way a text is viewed or understood can be called an interpretation, and can be made by literary critics (specialists in studying literary texts), reviewers, or everyday readers and students. It is about taking a position on particular elements of the text, or on what others say about it. For example you could consider:

1. Notions of 'character'

What **sort/type** of person Tess – or another character – is:

- Is the character an 'archetype' (a specific type of character with common features)? The critic Patricia Ingham has seen Tess as a new way of representing the common figure of the fallen woman. She is not only described as 'pure' by Hardy but she is also, according to Ingham, seen as 'a subject who desires'.
- Does the character personify, symbolise or represent a specific idea or trope ('the fallen woman?'; 'a symbol of modernity'; 'the tragic heroine'?)?
- Is the character modern, universal, of his/her time, historically accurate etc.? (For example, several of Tess's difficulties are caused by her status as a lower-class woman living in a poor, rural community. This setting is specific to a nineteenth-century world in which women were not treated equally to men and the rural poor were under pressure from social change and technological innovation.

EXAMINER'S TIP

Make sure you have thoroughly explored the different types of criticism written about *Tess of the D'Urbervilles*. Bear in mind that views of texts can change over time as values and experiences themselves change, and that criticism can be written for different purposes.

2. Ideas and issues

What the novel tells us about **certain ideas or issues** and how we interpret them. For example:

- How society is structured: we see that late Victorian society is very clearly marked by class division. Although Angel seems to overcome the divide between his middle-class background and the lower class milkmaids and farmers, his enlightened attitude is made to seem unusual amongst the middle classes. Hardy also shows us, however, that in the long term wealth and class are not stable, and high-class status can be lost as with the D'Urberville family from whom Tess descends.
- The role of men/women: in the latter part of the nineteenth century some women had started campaigning for better rights to education and work. However, the early feminist movement was mainly initiated by well-off women in cities. Tess is doubly disenfranchised by her status as a woman and as a member of a rural, working-class community.
- Moral codes and social justice: the novel makes us question our moral codes. Its protagonist is a murderer and yet we can still sympathise with, and even admire, her. The law is a distant force in this novel, Tess has no recourse to legal help when she is raped. Justice seems to be available to the wealthy and powerful, not to the impoverished and uneducated.

3. Links and contexts

To what extent the novel **links with, follows or pre-echoes** other texts and/or ideas. For example:

- Hardy tells the story of a fallen woman; he emphasises her purity and questions society's treatment of such women. Elizabeth Gaskell had earlier focused on the story of an unmarried mother in her novel *Ruth* (1853), which also directs readers' sympathises to its protagonist.

- The way Hardy uses rural Wessex in *Tess of the D'Urbervilles* to show the inevitable impact of modernising forces on rural lives can be compared to Laurie Lee's *Cider with Rosie* (1959). It too depicts a rural world on the cusp of change.
- In its discussion of spirituality and the loss of Christian faith, *Tess* could be compared with its near-contemporary novel, the best-selling *Robert Elsmere* (1888) by Mrs Humphry Ward.

4. Genre and narrative structure

How the novel is **constructed** and how Hardy **makes** his narrative:

- Does it follow particular narrative conventions? For example, those of the tragic genre?
- What are the functions of specific events, characters, plot devices, locations, etc. in relation to narrative or genre?
- What are the specific moments of tension, conflict, crisis and denouement – and do we agree on what they are?

5. Reader response and critical reaction

How the novel **works on the reader**, and whether this changes over time and in different contexts:

- How does Hardy **position** the reader? Are we to empathise with, feel distance from, judge and/or evaluate the events and characters?
- How do different readers view the novel – for example, different critics over time, or different readers in the 1890s in the US, postmodern and more recent years?

Writing about critical perspectives

The important thing to remember is that **you** are a critic too. Your job is to evaluate what a critic or school of criticism has said about the elements above, arrive at your own conclusions, and also express your own ideas.

In essence, you need to: **consider** the views of others, **synthesise** them, then decide on **your perspective**.

Explain the viewpoints

Critical view A about Hardy's Wessex:

> An eco-critical reading of 'Tess of the D'Urbervilles' would be interested in the ways in which rural traditions and farming methods are being displaced by technologies such as the threshing machine and steam engine.

Critical view B about the same aspect:

> A Marxist reading might use 'Tess of the D'Urbervilles' to shed light on ways in which Victorian society is structured around fixed and unequal class relations and would stress that the labour of the rural poor brings greater benefits to their employers than to themselves.

Then synthesise and add your perspective:

> We can gain insightful readings of 'Tess of the D'Urbervilles' from an ecocritical point of view by considering how the rural space of Wessex is being eroded by modern technologies, and also from a Marxist reading's focus upon the persistence of inequality in Victorian society. I think both suggest that Hardy's Wessex is a space in which Tess is trapped. Even though Hardy sometimes sees Tess as a figure of modernity she is still an 'unsophisticated girl' who looks 'foreign to the gleaming cranks and wheels' of the train. Hardy tells her story but insists that she cannot escape the gender and class constraints of her time and place.

A05 KEY INTERPRETATION

Here are just two examples of different kinds of response to *Tess of the D'Urbervilles*:

Critic 1 – Rosemarie Morgan's *Women and Sexuality in the Novels of Thomas Hardy* (1988) was one of the first critical texts to argue that Hardy was a feminist, and was particularly radical in his depiction of female sexuality.

Critic 2 – Jane Bownas, in *Thomas Hardy and Empire* (2012), argues that Hardy is fascinated with how his society understood the concepts of 'primitive' or 'civilised' and that his work is critical of the very notion of empire.

ANNOTATED SAMPLE ANSWERS

Below are extracts from three sample answers at different levels to the same task/question. Bear in mind that these responses may not correspond exactly to the style of question you might face (for example, AO5 is not assessed by Edexcel in relation to *Tess*), but they will give a broad indication of some of the key skills required.

> 'Tragedies can be shocking as much for their challenge to accepted ideas as for any violence they contain.'
>
> To what extent do you agree with this view in relation to two texts you have studied, bearing in mind the ways the writers have constructed their texts?

Candidate 1

AO1 *Clear opening, making specific reference to the text and weighing up possible readings*

In order to say how true this statement is in relation to Thomas Hardy's 'Tess of the D'Urbervilles', we must first consider which ideas Hardy is challenging. Hardy gave his book the subtitle 'a pure woman' in order to directly confront social expectations of female sexuality. We could argue, though, that by giving Tess a tragic ending, his challenge is not as forceful as it could be.

Tess is the eldest female child in a poor family and the expectation on her to help her family out of poverty through marriage marks the start of her tragedy. Her mother expects her to use her 'trump card', meaning her beautiful face, to hook Alec D'Urberville. What she doesn't take into account is that Alec is unlikely to treat a lower class woman with as much respect as he would a woman from a wealthy background like his own. In the late Victorian period when Hardy published Tess of the D'Urbervilles women were starting to argue for better rights but a poor young woman like Tess living in the countryside might not have even known about such developments. Gender and class inequality are both part of Tess's tragic story and Hardy takes issue with both.

AO3 *Uses some relevant context but could be more specific*

AO1 *Good reference to details of text*

It is hard to see how Tess's story could end in anything other than tragedy. The narrator constantly makes us feel as if Tess's fate is fixed and uses the novel's structure to emphasise this. Even when Tess seems to be at her happiest, when she is with Angel at Talbothays dairy, she constantly worries about her secret coming out and this shows a lack of confidence about how Angel will treat her. She almost tells him several times but cannot reveal her past until the wedding night. Angel's reaction to Tess's past is very harsh, especially when he admits his own sexual history. Hardy challenges the concept that men and women should be judged by different standards.

AO1 *A basic point, but a sign of critical thinking*

AO2 *Useful point but could expand to give an example of the mirroring structure in more specific terms*

AO2 *Good link back to the question*

If Tess was not so proud she might have escaped her tragic fate and could have carried on in her situation in life, helping her parents with their large family. Tess seems to have inherited her pride from her father who is proud of his aristocratic lineage, suggesting that pride is a universal characteristic regardless of class. This pride helps neither of the characters, Mr Durbeyfield is mocked for his delusions that his family could retain a prestigious place in society. Tess's pride keeps her from asking for help from Angel or his family when her situation becomes more and more difficult. Furthermore, pride also brings about

AO2 *Awareness of another narrative level*

some of the violence in the novel, for example when Tess strikes Alec with her glove and makes him bleed, prefiguring the later murder. Here Hardy shows us that pride, violence and tragedy are all linked in the character of Tess – despite her family's attempt to raise her up, death is the ultimate and shocking destiny for a girl like Tess, trapped by her class.

AO1 Well-worked point

AO1 Relates to the title but what follows retells the story rather than interpreting it

We could argue that Angel's story is also quite shocking. He challenges accepted ideas by not believing in God when the rest of his family are very religious. As a result his father will not send him to university and his position in life becomes very different from that of his brothers. He travels abroad where he, like many young men in the Victorian period, felt they might have a better chance in life. However, his journey to Brazil only ends in a near-death experience which ironically brings him to a more forgiving attitude towards Tess. You could also argue though that Angel is not a tragic hero as he is given another chance at happiness with Tess's sister, Liza-Lu. Tragic heroes like King Lear do not get second chances.

AO3 Relevant use of context, which might have been developed further with some specific details

AO4 Comparison with another text, but this is quite brief and does not directly address the question

As a reader, I felt much more sympathetic to Tess than to Angel. Although his attitude to her is very loving to begin with, the way in which he shifts his opinion when he finds out about her past made me question the strength of his love for her. Alec's love for Tess seems very strong, almost obsessive. He treats her violently by raping her in The Chase. He is not a tragic character, he is manipulative and aggressive and his wealth makes him feel that he is better than everyone else. He brings about Tess's tragedy, but we don't see him punished in the end.

AO1 Good critical approach; but this could be related more closely to the question

AO5 Needs developing, but basis of sound critical approach evident

In conclusion, Hardy does use 'Tess' to challenge social conventions concerning both gender and class. We know that some readers found this shocking at the time. For modern readers, it is not the depiction of female sexuality that seems shocking but the tragic unfairness and final violence with which Tess is treated.

AO3 Some knowledge of historical and critical context but this also needs developing

[The student then goes on to discuss the question in relation to *Death of a Salesman*.]

MID LEVEL

Comment

- AO1 A clear and methodical approach, but does not always keep a clear sense of the specific essay question in mind. Needs to push the analysis further to move it beyond broad observations and to make specific points in relation to the key terms of the question.
- AO2 Broad sense of ways in which meaning is shaped in *Tess of the D'Urbervilles*. Closer attention to language and technique would have raised the level of the analysis.
- AO3 Makes reference to historical context but critical engagement with it needs further development.
- AO4 Limited connections with other texts in this part of the question.
- AO5 This answer is marked by basic yet consistent critical evaluation, which demonstrates awareness of point of view. Doesn't engage with more sophisticated critical perspectives.

To improve the answer:

- Pay closer attention to the way meaning may be shaped by use of language and literary techniques. (AO2)
- Engage more purposefully with relevant historical and literary contexts. (AO3/AO4)
- Develop a more sophisticated understanding of how critical interpretations might shed light on key issues. (AO5)

Candidate 2

AO4 Broad literary connection

By calling his novel 'Tess of the D'Urbervilles', Hardy is inviting us to see the text as a bildungsroman – a popular form in the nineteenth century that told the story of the protagonist's education and growth to maturity. In these sorts of novels the character was usually given a happy ending – often in marriage. However, Hardy undercuts this expectation by turning his novel into a tragedy. Here, Hardy is challenging his reader's expectations of the novel. He also goes on to challenge restrictive ideas concerning class, gender and sexuality in Victorian Britain, in a way that was shocking for some of his readers at the time.

AO3 A broad sense of the social context of Victorian Britain

AO3 Strong opening to new paragraph and link to context

At the heart of the book is the attempt made by Tess to get out of the restricted social sphere into which she was born, and here Hardy makes an implicit critique of Britain's class system. She feels uneasy about 'claiming kin' with the D'Urbervilles but is not strong enough to resist her mother's persuasions, especially when she feels that the family's poverty is her fault after she accidentally kills the family's horse. She is also too naïve to say no to Alec's initial flirtations. She allows him to feed her strawberries and the reader gets the sense that she is, to some degree, attracted to him. Of course, Tess has received little formal education and doesn't understand the world well enough to challenge the confident middle-class figure of Alec. Again, we see Hardy presenting the injustice in the social system. Alec is not inherently better than Tess just because he is wealthier, in fact his morality is highly dubious.

AO1 Good understanding but could have given a quotation to develop further

The small moments of violence that we see in the text, such as when Tess snaps the shutter on Alec while he is talking to her through the window, foreshadow her tragic and shocking turn to violence at the end of the novel but they are not as significant as the constant challenge to society's structure that is inherent in the novel's very structure, and which we can see in Tess's tragic progression from innocent to fallen woman.

AO2 Useful relation of meaning to form

Tess is subject to violence, primarily from Alec. Alec is a predator who traps Tess and rapes her. As mentioned above, he has wealth and power, while she has neither. Near the end of the novel she says to Alec; 'O, you have torn my life all to pieces...made me a victim, a caged bird!' She blames Alec for her downfall and we might well agree. However, we could also argue that Tess is subject to violence from the narrator. From the very beginning of the novel the narrator's focus on her seems to target or even invade her. She becomes a sexual object in the narrator's eyes as much as she does for Alec. If even the narrator is against Tess, how can she hope to escape her fate? Perhaps this is where the real shock of the novel lies.

AO2 Crucial point

AO2 AO4 This is a really interesting point but would be better in a separate paragraph with further space for development

AO2
Alertness to Angel's role in the novel but this needs to link more clearly to the question

Angel is another character in the novel who has an effect on Tess. Angel meets Tess at Talbothays dairy and quickly comes to be infatuated by her. He wants to marry her even though his family background is very different; he comes from a middle-class background whereas her family are poor. Unlike Alec, whose intentions are negative, perhaps violent, from the start, this gives us hope that Tess will be raised above her station, to the position that her beauty and intelligence demand. However, the narrator tells us that Angel is in love with an idealised version of Tess, not Tess herself.

AO5
Broad literary connection which could be developed with more specific examples for the text

Throughout the text the two men are often compared, one seeming like an Angel and the other like a devil. We could argue that Tess is like Eve. She is tempted by Satan (in the form of Alec) and ends up falling from the garden of Eden into a world of sin and sorrow. Tess's punishment is death, and I would argue that it is all the more shocking because of Angel, and Hardy's, idealisation of Tess.

AO4
Useful comparison with text from the same genre

AO2
Good use of literary term

Finally, perhaps it is the lack of redemption that Hardy gives us at the end of his bildungsroman that is the most shocking. This can be compared to 'Jane Eyre' where Jane remains true to her faith and moral code through all her troubles, and Mr Rochester is redeemed for his sins through his marriage to Jane. There are moments when it seems that Tess could be happy, such as on her journey to Talbothays when Hardy gives us moments of pathetic fallacy by matching Tess's buoyant mood with the regeneration of nature in spring time. Ultimately, however, Tess is portrayed as the plaything of 'the President of the Immortals' – by this Hardy means that her fate is directed by a cruel higher power over which she has no control. She has no reward in life, and as readers we are left with a huge sense of loss and injustice. I would argue that the force of the novel is not a supernatural one, rather the higher power that controls Tess's violent ending is the social system that has allowed her to be treated with injustice and violence throughout her short life, and it is in this we see Hardy's challenge to accepted ideas.

[The student then goes on to discuss the question in relation to *Death of a Salesman*.]

GOOD LEVEL

Comment

- AO1 Places emphasis on Tess's role in the novel, and sets up a debate structure. The second half of the essay could have stayed more strongly on topic.
- AO2 The emphasis on Tess's role results in pertinent commentary on how Hardy constructs meaning through this character and the narrator.
- AO3 A broad sense of Victorian culture. Some specifics would have been useful.
- AO4 Interesting link to the *Bildungsroman* form, though more could have been done to link with other tragic genres or texts.
- AO5 The debate structure shows that the writer understands the ways in which the novel can be interpreted in different ways but an engagement with specific theories would be welcome.

To improve the answer:

- Tighten the argument in the second half so that it flows more smoothly. Signpost the links made between paragraphs. (AO1)
- Make more focused reference to historical and literary contexts. (AO3/AO4)
- Sharpen the sense of how a critical perspective shapes the interpretation of a text. (AO5)

Candidate 3

A01 The quotation offers a compelling hook into the essay and this introduction provides a strong central thesis

When Alec asks Tess if he loves her she replies in the negative: 'I have honour enough left, little as 'tis, not to tell that lie.' Tess is providing a shock to the moral conventions of the Victorian period. Hardy is suggesting that a poor, ill-educated fallen woman has a strong sense of honour and an unwavering moral code. This is a key part of Hardy's intention to show that Tess's fall is not caused by an innate character flaw. Rather, he makes it clear that the social conventions of the Victorian period entrap Tess and bring about her downfall. It is not necessarily the violence with which Tess's life is torn apart that is central to Hardy's book; it is the shock he wants to provide to his readers by making them consider the place of women in their society.

The nineteenth century was a period in which women were not treated equally with their male counterparts. They had less access to education and jobs, and were usually positioned in the domestic sphere as wife and mother. Women were expected to be 'angels of the house' (the title of a popular poem of the period). If women contravened these expectations of domesticity and purity they were treated harshly. Lower class women were particularly likely to suffer from gender discrimination and the Contagious Diseases Act (1864) made it legal for women to be locked up if suffering from venereal disease, while taking no action against men. Looking at 'Tess of the D'Urbervilles' from a feminist perspective makes this context particularly important to interpreting Tess's tragic fate and exploring the extent to which Hardy uses this as a medium to challenge accepted thinking.

A03 Historical context is specific and relevant

A01 Example of articulate, fluent expression throughout

Hardy makes it clear from very early on in the novel that Tess's gender is a key factor in the limitations placed on her life. She has ambitions to become a school teacher but she is needed to help her mother with domestic duties and childcare and this ambition is thwarted even before we meet Tess. She has little access to formal education but she also has little understanding of desire and sexuality when we first meet her. Hardy thus suggests that her social class makes her particularly liable to sexual violence; as she says to Alec, 'I didn't understand your meaning till it was too late.' Tess is in no position to defend herself against Alec. Feminist critics such as Rosemarie Morgan have defined Hardy himself as a feminist for bringing the harsh and unfair treatment of Tess to the forefront of his novel. In this reading Tess takes on metaphorical significance and stands for all women in Victorian society. It is also significant that she does violence to herself. On a literal level, she does violence to her beautiful face by trimming her eyebrows so as not to be exposed to further sexual depredation. On a metaphorical level, Tess sabotages her own hopes by refusing to ask for help from Angel's family because she feels so inadequate. She has internalised her society's limited expectations of both her gender and her class, with troublingly violent results.

A05 Confident use of specific critic in the correct critical context

A02 Appropriate quotation showing strong knowledge of the text

A02 Confident, in-depth analysis

Violence is enacted upon Tess at two central parts of the novel, the rape and the hanging. However, I would argue that, in a sense, these are not the most shocking parts of the novel, although they are the most brutal. In fact, the injustice with which Tess is treated by her new husband,

AO2 Very high level of language analysis

Angel, provides the novel's most profound shock. When she tells him about her past he only laughs coldly and says, 'Forgiveness does not apply to the case. You were one person; now you are another.' He makes his volte face because he judges her by different standards because she is a woman. His language is cold and unemotional and the second sentence emphasises the split he sees in Tess by using a construction split by a caesura. His words seem to obliterate Tess's very identity; she becomes almost completely passive, offering no defence. Alec may have used literal violence on Tess, but Angel's words cause a violent cataclysm in her sense of self.

AO5 An apposite critical viewpoint that allows the writer to make an even more complex point

It is worth mentioning here that Hardy's ability to shock his readers was hampered by censorship when Tess was first published in serial form in The Graphic magazine. In this earlier edition Hardy's ability to shock his readers is compromised, however, in the volume edition Hardy reinstated such material that represented sexual desire in women. Margaret Elvy has argued in 'Sexing Hardy: Thomas Hardy and Feminism' that Hardy 'recognised the importance of erotic desire in fiction'. His novel moves away from representations of women as domestic and asexual to show that women are sexual beings. In doing so he attempts to redefine his society's understanding of purity by calling Tess a 'pure woman', which clearly represented a challenge to the conventions of the time.

AO3 Strong understanding of publishing context and of differing interpretations on offer in the different versions of Tess

Even the violence that Tess commits at the book's tragic finale is brought about by, and pales in comparison with, the shocking injustice of the treatment she receives as a woman. When Angel returns it becomes clear that Tess only gave in to Alec's demands when he exerted powerful emotional blackmail, playing on the expectation that she will help her family as a woman would be expected to: 'My little sisters and brothers and my mother's needs – they were the things you moved me by'. Even at the end she cannot escape her role as daughter and sister.

AO2 Excellent choice of quotation, well analysed

AO3 Appropriate analysis of literary context, making reference to the tragedy genre

Finally, the domestic violence we encounter in Hardy's novel is very different to the violence that we might find in a Shakespearean tragedy such as 'Hamlet'. In Jacobean and Elizabethan tragedies the protagonist (and antagonists) invariably meet violent deaths on stage. However, Tess's murder of Alec and her own death are only seen from distanced perspectives.

[The student then goes on to discuss the question in relation to *Death of a Salesman*.]

VERY HIGH LEVEL

Comment

- AO1 An impressively coherent and well-argued response. In control of materials and constructs of a persuasive argument.
- AO2 Use of quotations has a confidence that reflects an assured grasp of ways in which meaning is shaped in the text.
- AO3 Focused and highly specific engagement with historical context, clearly related back to the text.
- AO4 Secondary literary and critical materials used with precision and purpose.
- AO5 Astute and assured reference to feminist critics and the light they might shed on central issues of the text.

PRACTICE TASK

Now it's your turn to work through an exam-style task on *Tess of the D'Urbervilles*. The key is to:

● Quickly read and decode the task/question

● Briefly plan your points – then add a few more details, such as evidence, or make links between them

● Write your answer

Decode the question

> 'All tragic fiction is based on the creation of suspense.' To what extent do you agree with this view in relation to Tess of the D'Urbervilles, in terms of how it is constructed by its writer?

'All tragic fiction ... suspense'	suggests that a common element in tragic fiction is 'suspense', despite the tragic ending
'suspense'	relates to a sense of being uncertain about what will happen. This sense may provoke excitement, fear or pleasure in a reader.
'To what extent do you agree?'	What is my view? Do I agree with the statement completely, partially or not at all?
'constructed by its writer'	What has Hardy done that supports (or doesn't support) this idea?

EXAMINER'S TIP

Remember to incorporate the views of critics, but make sure that the central idea is your own!

Plan and write

● Decide your viewpoint

● Plan your points

● Think of key evidence and quotations

● Write your answer

Once you have finished, use the **Mark scheme** on page 103 to evaluate your response.

Success criteria

● Show your understanding of the idea of tragedy as a genre

● Draw on a range of critical views or different interpretation as appropriate

● Sustain your focus on the idea of 'suspense'

● Argue your **point of view** clearly and logically

● Make perceptive points and express your ideas confidently

● Support your points with relevant, well-chosen evidence including quotations

● Use literary terminology accurately and appropriately with reference to the effect on the reader

● Write in fluent, controlled and accurate English

FURTHER READING

John Alcorn, *The Nature Novel from Hardy to Lawrence*, Macmillan, 1977

Diana Basham, *The Trial of Woman: Feminism and the Occult Sciences in Victorian Literature and Society*, Macmillan, 1992

Gillian Beer, *Darwin's Plots: Evolutionary Narrative in Darwin, George Eliot and Nineteenth-Century Fiction*, second edition, Cambridge University Press, 2000

William Davis, *Thomas Hardy and the Law: Legal Presences in Hardy's Life and Fiction,* University of Delaware Press, 2002

Tim Dolin and Peter Widdowson, *Thomas Hardy: Contemporary Literary* Studies, Palgrave Macmillan, 2004.

Ralph W. V. Elliott, *Thomas Hardy's English*, Basil Blackwell, 1986

Margaret Elvy, *Sexing Hardy: Thomas Hardy and Feminism*, Crescent Moon Publishing, 2007

Marjorie Garson, *Hardy's Fables of Integrity: Woman, Body, Text*, Clarendon Press, 1991

Simon Gatrell, *Thomas Hardy and the Proper Study of Mankind*, Macmillan, 1993

James Gibson, ed., *Thomas Hardy: Interviews and Recollections*, Macmillan, 1999

John Goode, 'Woman and the Literary Text' in Juliet Mitchell and Ann Oakley, eds., *The Rights and Wrongs of Women*, Penguin, 1976

John Goode, *Thomas Hardy, The Offensive Truth*, Blackwell, 1988

G. Harvey and N. Tredell, eds., *Thomas Hardy: Tess of the D'Urbervilles*, Palgrave Macmillan, 2002

J. Hillis Miller, *Fiction and Repetition: Seven English Novels*, Basil Blackwell, 1982
    See his chapter 'Tess of the D'Urbervilles: Repetition as Immanent Design'

Alun Howkins, *Reshaping Rural England: A Social History 1850–1925*, HarperCollins, 1991

A. M. Jackson, *Illustration and the Novels of Thomas Hardy*, Rowman and Littlefield, 1981

James R. Kincaid, *Child-Loving: The Erotic Child and Victorian Culture*, Routledge, 1992

Dale Kramer, *The Cambridge Companion to Thomas Hardy*, Cambridge University Press, 2006

N. Lacey, *Women, Crime and Character: From Moll Flanders to Tess of the D'Urbervilles*, Oxford University Press, 2008

J. T. Laird, *The Shaping of Tess of the D'Urbervilles*, Oxford University Press, 1975
    For an account of the formation of the novel

Phillip Mallett, *Thomas Hardy: Texts and Contexts*, Palgrave Macmillan, 2002

Michael McKeon, ed., *Theory of the Novel: A Historical Approach*, Johns Hopkins University Press, 2000

Kevin Moore, *The Descent of the Imagination: Post-Romantic Culture in the Later Novels of Thomas Hardy*, New York University Press, 1990

Rosemarie Morgan, *Women and Sexuality in the Novels of Thomas Hardy*, Routledge, 1988

Rosemarie Morgan, *The Ashgate Research Companion to Thomas Hardy*. Ashgate, 2010

Ross C. Murfin, *Swinburne, Hardy, Lawrence and the Burden of Belief*, University of Chicago Press, 1978

Jeff Nunokawa, 'Tess, tourism, and the spectacle of the woman' in Linda M. Shires, ed., *Rewriting the Victorians: Theory, History and the Politics of Gender*, Routledge, 1992

Francis O'Gorman, ed., *The Victorian Novel*, Blackwell, 2002

H. P. Owen, *Concepts of Deity*, Macmillan, 1971

Toni Reed, *Demon-Lovers and Their Victims in British Fiction*, University Press of Kentucky, 1988

Harriet Ritvo, *The Animal Estate: The English and Other Creatures in Victorian England*, Penguin, 1990

K. D. M. Snell, *Annals of the Labouring Poor: Social Change and Agrarian England, 1660–1900*, Cambridge University Press, 1987

Rebecca Stott, *The Fabrication of the Late-Victorian Femme Fatale: The Kiss of Death*, Macmillan, 1992
    For an account of Hardy's self-censorship

J. A. Sutherland, *Victorian Novelists and Publishers*, Athlone Press, 1976

Tony Tanner, 'Colour and Movement in Hardy's *Tess of the D'Urbervilles*' in Ian Watt, ed., *The Victorian Novel, Modern Essays in Criticism*, Oxford University Press, 1971

Herbert F. Tucker, ed., *A Companion to Victorian Literature and Culture*, Blackwell, 1999

Judith Weissman, *Half Savage and Hardy and Free: Women and Rural Radicalism in the Nineteenth-Century Novel*, Wesleyan University Press, 1987

Merryn Williams, *Thomas Hardy and Rural England*, Macmillan, 1972

Raymond Williams, *The Country and the City*, Oxford University Press, 1973

Raymond Williams, *The English Novel from Dickens to Lawrence*, Hogarth, 1984

LITERARY TERMS

anthropomorphic human attributes ascribed to something that is not human

closure the feeling of completeness and finality achieved by the ending of some literary works; especially associated with the classic **realist** texts of the nineteenth century

defamiliarisation 'making strange'; Hardy's writing can often strip away everything that is familiar about the world, so that we see it anew. This can be referred to as estrangement or defamiliarisation

denouement final unfolding of the plot

dialect a non-standard mode of speech related to a particular geographical area. Hardy conveys the lives of his rural characters through their use of west country dialect

ecocritical an interpretation of a literary text that focuses on the ways in which the environment is represented by the author

expository from 'exposition', i.e. an explanation, or to do with the delivery of information

flashback narrative technique that disrupts time sequence by introducing an event or memory which happened in the past prior to the present action of the novel

foreshadow prefigure a later event or turning point. This literary technique is used extensively by Hardy

free indirect discourse a style of third-person narration that expresses the character's voice without an introductory expression like 'she said' or 'she thought', thereby making it more direct and powerful

Gothic a popular form that emerged in the eighteenth century; during the nineteenth century Gothic went through an architectural and stylistic revival that was often linked to medievalism. In literary form, its eerie and fantastic devices were often used in sensation fiction and other popular Victorian genres

irony covert sarcasm; saying one thing while meaning another; using words to convey the opposite of their literal meaning; saying something that has one meaning for someone knowledgeable about a situation and another meaning for those who are not; incongruity between what might be expected and what actually happens; ill-timed arrival of an event which had been hoped for

juxtaposition bringing two oppositional terms or concepts together to present a contrast

melodramatic a melodrama was originally a popular play with music which aimed to excite the audience through incident and strong but simple feelings, and with characters who were clearly 'good' or 'bad' and an ending that was always happy

metaphorical from metaphor – figure of speech in which a descriptive term, or name or action characteristic of one object is applied to another to suggest a likeness between, but which does not use 'like' or 'as' in the comparison

metaphysical to do with the immaterial, or philosophy that there is something beyond or independent of the human; the abstract, sometimes the supernatural

naturalism a form of **realism** emphasising the everyday and even the sordid in its representation of human life

objectified made into, or looked at, as an object or image; made into a spectacle

omniscient narrator storyteller with total, God-like knowledge of the characters and their actions

pastoral literature about an idealised rural life. Written from the **point of view**, but also often critical, of the city. The implication is that rural life is simpler and more wholesome than urban life

pathetic fallacy a literary trope that represents the non-human (nature, the weather, animals, things) as having human emotions

pathos suffering feeling; that quality in a work of art that arouses pity and sadness

point of view seen from the viewpoint or through the eyes of a particular character

psychomachea a medieval morality play in which vice and virtue battle for the soul of Everyman. Derived from a poem by Prudentius, 'Psychomachia', *c*.400, which in the Greek means 'a struggle or fight for life'

queer theory a diverse field of interpretation that involves questioning the fixity of identity, particularly with regards to gender and sexuality

realist a realist author represents the world as it is rather than as it should be, using description rather than invention; observes and documents everyday life in straightforward prose; draws on characters from all levels of society, but often from the lowest classes; represents their speech and manners accurately. Realism became the dominant form of literature in the nineteenth century

subjectivity the 'subject' is used in a specialised way here to refer to the individual as understood in western capitalist society. Individuals possess subjectivity, in the sense of feeling and thinking freely and independently, but they are also 'subjected', in the sense of being in abeyance to authority: they are politically 'subject', i.e. not really free at all

synaesthesia the triggering of one sense (e.g. smell) by another (e.g. vision)

tragedy originally a form of ancient Greek drama, now more broadly refers to a text or plot that emphasises suffering and often death

verisimilitude giving the appearance of truth or reality

REVISION TASK ANSWERS

Revision Task 1: Moments of foreboding

- The spotlight on Tess in Chapter 2 where her blood-red ribbon highlights her in contrast to the other young women.
- The D'Urberville legend, such as the coach that seems to prefigure tragedy and even murder.
- The tone becomes particularly eerie at moments that are heavily laden with foreboding, such as the last few chapters of Phase the Fourth.

Revision Task 2: Directing the scene

- Dark lighting could be used to convey the night-time situation and Tess's bleak outlook.
- Tess being covered in Prince's blood would be shocking, but could be effected in a stylised way to avoid the overtones of a horror movie.
- Background music could be used to convey a change of pace and perspective.

Revision Task 3: Tess's faith

- Tess is embittered by the fact that Sorrow cannot be buried in consecrated ground.
- She feels tortured by the sign painter and the biblical slogans that seem to be targeted directly at her.
- Tess and Angel do have different spiritual outlooks; ultimately he cannot offer her the hope that they will meet in heaven, but she is still consoled by her own belief, in Chapter 58.

Revision task 4: Gender constructs

- When Angel idealises Tess, we are meant to see it as a warning that he does not truly know her.
- Tess is beautiful but Hardy emphasises that she is an ordinary woman and draws connections between his protagonist and the other women in the text, notably Izz Huett and 'Liza-Lu.
- Angel and Alec both experience heterosexual desire but their ways of expressing this aspect of their masculinity are different. Alec uses force, Angel does not.

Revision task 5: Visual distance

- Tess is seen by Angel from a distance when he looks back at the dancing in Chapter 2.
- In Chapter 16 Tess is described 'like a fly on a billiard table', making her seem insignificant in comparison to the natural world.
- The most pathetic scene in the novel is when Tess's hanging is watched from a distance by Angel and 'Liza-Lu.

Revision task 6: The impact of modernity

- The reaping machine in Chapter 14.
- The train in Chapter 30.
- The threshing machine in Chapter 47.
- The quick succession of events in the modern town of Sandbourne seems to suggest time moving more quickly than at other moments in the text.

Revision task 7: Angel's love for Tess

- There are several references to Eden in the courtship at Talbothays.
- Angel likens her to classical and mythical figures. She prefers to be called Tess.
- He tries to shape his ideal Tess by dressing her in new clothes and educating her.

Revision task 8: Sexual morality

- Joan Durbeyfield's attitude to her daughter's sexual past is forgiving and she recommends that Tess keep her secret to herself.
- Tess pleads, 'Forgive me as you are forgiven! I forgive you, Angel' (p. 228), making Angel's attitude seem all the more unfair and callous.
- In telling Angel of her past, Tess seems to have fallen from her earlier idealised position – Angel's reaction could not be more stark or unforgiving.

Revision task 9: The role of fate

- Jack and Joan Durbeyfield are trapped by their poverty and are unable to escape from it by their own efforts or by using Tess.
- Tess's limited education traps her in her social class.
- The D'Urberville legend seems to haunt Tess at key moments, such as when she seems to hear the coach or when she spends her wedding night in the ancient family mansion.

Revision task 10: Character and landscape

- Tess's first experience of the valley in which Talbothays is situated (Chapter 16) reflects her renewed energy and optimism at this stage in the novel.
- The Durbeyfield family home is in a small village called Marlott. It is remote from large towns and is suggestive of the family's lack of connection with those outside their social class.
- Tess's removal to Sandbourne with Alec is suggestive of her emotional distance from her past life at this late stage in the novel.

PROGRESS CHECK ANSWERS

Part Two: Studying *Tess of the D'Urbervilles*

Section One: Check your understanding

1. In what ways is Tess disadvantaged by her background? Make a list of four or five reasons outlined early on in the novel.

- Tess is the eldest child and is expected to help her mother with the domestic duties of the household.
- Tess's education was curtailed and her ambition to be a teacher forestalled.
- Tess's mother and father do not plan for their family's long-term well-being.
- Tess has little understanding of sex and her innocence is a disadvantage. She asks her mother 'Why didn't you warn me?'.

2. Make a table contrasting rural life with the modern world as it is glimpsed in the novel.

- Rural life is slow and determined by the rhythms of nature.
- Modernity speeds up the pace of life, as symbolised by the train that whisks the Talbothays milk up to London.
- In rural life the labourer is strongly connected to the land.
- The modern farm machinery that Tess encounters at Flintcomb-Ash.

3. List three moments in the narrative that shed light on the character of Angel Clare.

- The first time we meet Angel in Chapter 2 he is differentiated from his brothers and we are told that he has an instinctive reaction to Tess.
- Angel's reaction to Tess's revelation of her past sexual encounter shows that Angel is conventional in his expectations of female behaviour and demonstrates a level of hypocrisy.
- Angel's sleep-walking episode in Chapter 37 reveals how he feels about Tess on a subconscious level.

4. Consider two or three of the minor characters in the novel and list their functions in terms of supporting the development of the plot or the development of other characters.

- Izz Huett provides a foil to Tess. She is the most similar to Tess of all the dairymaids and when Angel asks her to accompany him to Brazil her reaction is crucial to the plot. Angel goes alone.
- Retty's attempted suicide helps to precipitate Tess's confession.
- Mercy Chant demonstrates the difference between Angel and his parents. They deem her a suitable wife; Angel does not warm to her type of Christianity.

5. List three or four significant social changes Hardy examines in the novel and consider how they affect rural life.

- Tess received a better education than her parents; throughout the nineteenth century education increased in availability, particularly to the urban poor, leading towards the 1870 and 1891 Education Acts.
- Sandbourne, the seaside town where Angel finds Tess, is a new urban development and seems to have sprung up from the countryside, disturbing the landscape that had remained unchanged for thousands of years.
- Emigration was a possibility for some nineteenth-century farmers; Angel tries it but finds it more problematic than he expected.

6. What is the significance of machines in *Tess of the D'Urbervilles*? Give at least two examples.

- In Chapter 30 we see Angel and Tess delivering the milk to the railway station. The spread of the train network connected rural areas to large cities with much greater speed than ever before.
- In Chapter 47 we see the threshing machine in action. The industrial revolution and the development of steam-powered farm machinery began to displace some forms of intensive manual labour, although the machine still requires intensive work from Tess in particular.

7. Identify three of Tess's solitary journeys and briefly consider the significance of each.

- Tess's journey from her family home to Trantridge to 'claim kin' with the D'Urbervilles is the first time she leaves the Vale of Blackmoor which has previously made up 'to her the world' (p. 36).
- In Chapter 16 Tess walks to Talbothays in the 'valley of the Great Dairies'. This marks a resurgence and renewal in her life.
- Tess's journey to Flintcomb-Ash is hard, dreary and lonely. She even ties up her face with a handkerchief and snips off her eyebrows to fend off attention.

8. Make a table offering points of comparison between Angel and Alec. Think about both similarities and differences.

- Angel is angelic and plays a harp; Alec appears as devilish.

- Angel's love is spiritual; Alec's is material.
- Angel is physically attractive; Alec has 'an almost swarthy complexion, with full lips … above which was a well-groomed black moustache with curled points' (p. 40).
- Both men think of taking Tess abroad.
- Both dress Tess up in fine clothes and try to turn her into something she is not.

9. Write a paragraph on what you find interesting about the depiction of the natural environment in Hardy's novel.

- Nature is sometimes personified. For example, at the beginning of Chapter 14 the sun 'had a curious sentient, personal look'.
- Sometimes Tess is shown to be part of nature: 'she was of a piece with the element she moved in.' (p. 85)
- At other times nature seems hostile to the protagonist, such as when the mist seems to collude in Alec's plans to disorientate Tess and take advantage of her.

10. Consider three of the letters written in the novel. What are their functions and what do they reveal about their writers?

- In Chapter 31 Joan Durbeyfield's letter urges that Tess keep her past a secret from Angel. Tess takes her mother's advice to heart.
- Tess tries writing to Angel several times and eventually manages to write a passionate plea in Chapter 48 that reveals the insecurity of her social and emotional position as a married woman with no husband.
- Marian and Izz write an anoymous letter to Angel in Chapter 52. They suggest Tess needs her husband to return as she is in danger. This letter maintains the sisterly bonds between the women.

11. Why are animals significant in this text? Give three examples of different animals used by Hardy.

- Prince, the horse, is vital to the Durbeyfield family business. His death sets off the train of events that put Tess in Alec's power.
- The cows at Talbothays are treated as individuals with preferences for different milkers. Their gentle presence provides the backdrop to Angel and Tess's courtship.
- Tess feels for the suffering birds as if they were 'kindred sufferers' in Chapter 41 (p. 279).

12. List three moments when the narration becomes distanced or detached and think about why Hardy might adjust the perspective of the novel at key moments.

- Chapter 2 sees Hardy introducing Tess. Tess only comes in to focus as an individual after Hardy has introduced her as part of a group.
- We see Tess's reaction to Angel's reappearance through the limited and detached perspective of Mrs Brooks

looking through the keyhole. It is through this minor character's eyes that we also discover Alec's body.
- The final moments of the novel look upon Angel and 'Liza-Lu as 'two speechless gazers' (p. 398). Moments when individual names are not used might make us think about the way that individual stories connect to more universal issues.

13. List three instances of violent action in *Tess of the D'Urbervilles* and comment on each.

- Prince is killed by 'the pointed shaft of the cart' (p. 33). Not only does his death lead directly to Tess claiming kin with the D'Urbervilles, we could also argue that this violent penetration prefigures Tess's rape.
- Tess lets the window fall on Alec's arm in Chapter 51 when he is pressing her to bring her homeless family to Trantridge. We are not sure whether or not Tess does this on purpose.
- Tess's murder of Alec is of couse the most obviously violent act in the novel but it also leads to the taking of Tess's own life through a legal form of violence, her hanging.

14. How is love represented in the novel? Write a paragraph considering imagery, symbolism and dialogue.

- Alec couches his interest in Tess in very colloquial, material terms. This is reflected in his dialogue: he calls her 'my pretty Coz' (p. 41) and 'artful hussy' (p. 57).
- Angel's love for Tess is also physical and he embraces her in Chapter 27 while they are skimming the milk. Tess and Angel's courtship is very intimately bound up with the setting of the dairy at Talbothays.
- Tess's love for Angel seems much more constant than his for her. She idealises him and writes to him, 'Angel I live entirely for you' (p. 336). In some senses her love is self-sacrificing.

15. Make a table listing three or four events that happen in the second half of the novel and the ways in which they are foreshadowed in the first half.

- Tess eventually becomes Alec's mistress and we might argue that this is foreshadowed from very early on when, for example, Tess allows him to feed her a strawberry (p. 42).
- Jack Durbeyfield's death in Chapter 50 is foreshadowed in Chapter 3 when Joan tells us of the 'fat around his heart' (p. 22) and also by his tendency to look back to his long-deceased ancestors rather than into the future of his own family.
- Tess's sorrowful journey to Flintcomb-Ash has a more joyful counterpart earlier in the novel when she walks to Talbothays. The closing down of possibilities for happiness echoes the larger structure of the tragedy.

16. How is the impact of rural depopulation felt in this novel? Make a list.

- The class to which Tess's 'father and mother had belonged' (p. 352) including carpenters, shoemakers and blacksmiths rather than farm labourers, are being pushed out and making village life less varied.
- Both Alec and Angel consider emigrating, Angel to Brazil and Alec to Africa to work as a missionary.
- Tess and Angel encounter untenanted spaces in the text. Both the 'mouldy old habitation' where they spend their wedding night (p. 216) and the empty manor-house they stumble upon in Chapter 57 speak of a loss of rural inhabitants.

17. Think about the three key families in this novel: the Durbeyfields, the Clares and the D'Urbervilles. Make a table outlining contrasts and comparisons.

- The Durbeyfields are represented in a trajectory of descent from their noble ancestry to their current humble situation. The parents are improvident and the children are not well-defined characters: Tess stands out amongst them.
- The middle-class Clares are a more stable family. Angel is the outsider as a non-believer in a family of devout Christians.
- The D'Urberville family is affluent, with their money and their family name coming through success in trade. Alec and his mother do not demonstrate the loving familial bonds we see elsewhere in the novel.

18. Why is work so significant in this novel? Write a short paragraph explaining your answer.

- Work gives Tess a sense of purpose, agency and enjoyment at Talbothays.
- But when machines start to intervene in farm work, Tess's relationship to the natural world shifts and the monotony of her work seems to be part of her oppressive fate. See, for example, Tess working with the turnip-slicing machine in Chapter 46.
- Jack Durbeyfield's lack of interest in work demonstrates his improvidence and means that his daughter must take his place as a provider for the family.

19. List four or five ways in which the present is haunted by the past in Hardy's novel.

- Tess's acts of remembrance for her baby, tending and placing flowers on his grave.
- Parson Tringham brings the past back into the lives of the Durbeyfields through his antiquarian research.
- Ancient traditions or pagan beliefs continue to work on the lives of modern individuals, such as the ill-omened meaning of the cross upon which Alec makes Tess swear she will not tempt him, in Chapter 45.

- The buildings and physical structures of the past continue into the present. Ancient humanity is recalled in Stonehenge and the incremental geological changes that form Tess's natural environment continue into the present.

20. Consider the moments in the novel where we are invited to think about families and heredity. List both the positive and negative qualities that might have been passed down to Tess through her family.

- Tess's life is haunted by her ancestral lineage. We see this particularly when she finds herself at the D'Urberville tomb in Chapter 52.
- Tess's features seem to have been passed down from her ancestors, although the portraits of the women in the D'Urberville mansion (Chapter 34) are grotesque inversions of Tess's beauty.
- We should not forget that Tess has two parents and although we assume her mother's heritage is more humble, Joan Durbeyfield asserts that Tess inherits her beauty from her mother, at the end of Chapter 6. We are told that Tess has the 'energy of her mother's unexpended family' (p. 104) in Chapter 16.

Section Two: Working towards the exam

1. *Tess of the D'Urbervilles* is a story about the relationship between the individual and their hostile environment. Discuss.

- Tess's family environment is difficult and the Durbeyfields seem to create problems, such as their broken roof, through their improvidence. This environment continues to draw Tess back in order to try to help her family, to the detriment of her own self-fulfiment.
- The natural world sometimes seems to conspire against Tess, such as when the mist provides cover for Alec's rape.
- Tess often seems alone, particularly on her journeys across the countryside, which are frequently lengthy and tiring.
- In Angel's relationship with his brothers we are told that 'his squareness would not fit the round hole that had been prepared for him' (p. 165). We might read this to illuminate the situation of all the individuals of the novel as fundamentally alienated from each other.
- The technology we encounter in the novel seems to make Tess's environment alien and hostile to her. See the turnip-slicing machine in Chapter 46.

2. Does Hardy's novel criticise inequality? If so, how and why?

- Yes, the double standard by which women's sexuality is judged is condemned. This is reinforced by Angel's admission of what we see as an equivalent sexual history. The reader cannot sympathise with his hypocrisy.

- The life of the rural labourer is shown to be difficult and unstable in comparison to the lives of those further up the social scale.
- The narrator, however, does sometimes seem to look down upon or patronise Tess, which compromises the critique of inequality.

3. How far do you agree with the idea that Tess's fate could only ever be tragic?

- Tess is a proud character; her pride is part of her tragic downfall.
- Tess is linked inextricably to her D'Urberville heritage, which is always associated with tragic or ominous fates.
- Once Tess has lost her virginity, in the eyes of her community she will always be a 'fallen' or 'impure' woman and her fate will necessarily be tragic.
- However, the significant tragedies of Tess's life are caused by other people: Alec's rape and Angel's abandonment.
- There are moments of hope, such as Tess's journey to Talbothays, where it seems possible that Tess's fate might be more hopeful.

4. How is the novel's concern with the passage of time reflected in its structure?

- The novel is divided into phases that all reflect significant movements across both time and space.
- The novel depicts the passage of time through changes in the seasons and weather.
- Events or characters that we first see early in the novel are often repeated or mirrored later on, such as the appearance of Car Darch at Trantridge and later at Flintcomb-Ash. This gives a sense of time as cyclical or repetitive.

5. What is the relationship between religion and morality in *Tess of the D'Urbervilles*?

- Hardy's views on religion are complex. Although he lost his own faith he was respectful of Christianity and recognised its link with morality.
- Alec finds religion but later goes on to see his religious zeal as a 'craze' (p. 356). But he abandons his morally respectful attitude to Tess when he abandons his religious beliefs.
- Mr Clare's religious belief seems to consider self-sacrifice an important part of his and his family's morality.
- Tess seems to have an innate sense of right and wrong that is independent of any religious belief.
- The signpainter's biblical messages represent a very black and white understanding of religious morality, which Tess finds cruel.

···
Part Three: Characters and themes
············

Section One: Check your understanding
···

1. Write a list of four or five ways in which minor characters impact upon the trajectories of the central plot.

- Cuthbert and Felix Clare are overheard lamenting Angel's marriage in Chapter 44.
- Tess feels that the whole Clare family is set against her and doesn't return to ask Angel's parents for help.
- Farmer Groby turns out to have been the man who insulted Tess at the inn in Chapter 33. His words increase Tess's feelings of guilt and anxiety as the wedding approaches.
- When Angel asks Izz Huett to go with him to Brazil in Chapter 40, her answer defending Tess's love for him lays the foundations for his ultimate return.

2. Locate a passage of dialogue between Tess and Alec and one between Tess and Angel. Compare the ways in which Tess's lovers speak to her and what their conversation reveals about their attitudes to their beloved.

- Alec and Tess's dialogue on pp. 76–7 suggests his disrespectful attitude towards her and contains hints of her later violence.
- On pp. 123–4 Angel listens to Tess and respectfully asks for her opinions and thoughts. At this point in their relationship it is interesting to note that Tess still calls Angel 'sir'.

3. 'A weakness of this novel is that neither Angel or Alec are truly believable characters.' Do you agree with this statement?

- Yes: The extremity and hypocrisy of Angel's reaction to Tess's admission of her sexual history is not believable.
- Yes: Alec's conversion to pious Christianity seems very brief and he is easily swayed when he encounters Tess again.
- No: Angel's reaction to Tess's admission reflects the double standard by which female sexuality was judged in comparison to male sexuality.
- No: Alec's conversion and loss of faith gives him a sense of development as a character and sets up an important contrast with Angel.

4. Make a table offering three or four comparisons of the cruelties of nature versus the benevolence of nature.

- The natural world, and a particularly fine spring help to revive Tess after her trauma (p. 99).
- Talbothays is a place of plenty, represented by the milk, cheese and other food provided by the Cricks from their farm.

- The climate in Brazil is said to have been part of the cause of Angel's illness and the death of his un-named companion.
- The freezing winter at Flintcomb-Ash pushes Tess to the limits of her physical endurance and sees Marian drinking alcohol to alleviate her situation.

5. What is the thematic significance of ruined or dilapidated buildings in the novel?

- Tess frequently finds herself in ruinous buildings, from the thatched cottage over-run by chickens at The Slopes to Stonehenge in the final scenes of the novel. These ruins suggest the persistence of the past in the present but also simultaneously emphasise the degrading effects of time.

6. How does Tess's story show gender to be a significant issue? List three events and briefly explain the significance of each.

- Tess's pregnancy and brief life as a mother. Although the narrator passes over this period fairly quickly, it is of course significant that because of her gender Tess must carry and care for the illegitimate child, whereas Alec can walk away.
- In Chapter 52 we are told that because Tess's family is only made up of women and children, they are superfluous to the requirements of any employer.
- The difference between Angel's reaction to Tess's admission of a past sexual encounter and her reaction to his admission of an equivalent situation demonstrates a biased attitude towards female sexuality.

7. Make a list of three ways in which religious faith is problematised in the novel.

- Felix and Cuthbert Clare are unsympathetic characters from the very start of the novel. They represent a scholarly and hierarchical attitude to faith.
- Angel Clare has lost his faith.
- Alec's conversion to Christianity seems brief and hollow.

8. Identify three types of love found in the novel and give an example of each.

- Motherly love: Seen in Tess's love for Sorrow, her grief at his death and her later tending of his grave.
- Obsessive or idealising love: Both Alec and Angel return to Tess's image obsessively. Alec's 'love' may be better described as desire, however.
- Love within marriage: Seen between Tess and Angel in the final sections of the novel.

9. Write one or two paragraphs discussing the idea that in the world of the novel justice is possible for men but not for women.

- Men of the privileged classes, such as Alec and Angel, have power over Tess. Her fate is ultimately controlled by them.

- Tess has no recourse to legal or other assistance following her rape. Alec's later offers to provide her with money are insulting.
- In the Victorian period laws were decided and enacted by men to the frequent disadvantage of women (e.g. The Contagious Diseases Act took action against women, not men, in attempting to cut down prostitution).

10. Give an example of pathetic fallacy in the novel and explain its significance.

- The mist in Chapter 11 is symbolic of Tess's bewildered and vague state of mind. It provides conditions that enable Alec to rape Tess.

Section Two: Working towards the exam

1. Compare the representation of women in *Tess of the D'Urbervilles* with the way in which female characters are presented in any of the other texts you have studied.

- *Wuthering Heights,* like *Tess,* provides us with examples of women who are not middle-class or urban. The settings are rural and relatively isolated for these women.
- Both texts are intergenerational and consider relationships between mothers and their children.
- Sexual desire is represented in both Cathy and Tess's characters, which is relatively unusual for Victorian novels.
- Although Nelly Dean has some control over the narrative in *Wuthering Heights*, the women in both novels are represented by male narrators.

2. 'Tess embodies a clash between nature and society.' Do you agree?

- Yes, Tess is seen as a 'child of nature'.
- Tess is often in harmony with her natural surroundings. She feels comfortable working in the rural, natural world.
- She presents a contrast to modern society as represented by Sandbourne.
- The role of Sorrow is also interesting with regards to this clash between nature and society, regarding the social stigma of illegitimacy.

3. Discuss the ways in which Hardy's narrator seeks to represent an unequal and unjust society.

- The women of the text have fewer opportunities than the men, although class and wealth are also factors here regarding the possibilities open to Angel and Alec.
- Tess's education is curtailed because she is from a lower-class family and her help is needed at home.
- Tess sees injustice as fundamental to life, for example when she tells Abraham that they are living in a 'blighted' world.
- Hardy doesn't necessarily provide any solutions for social injustice, but it is significant that he flags it up for his readers.

Part Four: Genre, structure and language

Section One: Check your understanding

1. List three ways in which we might define Tess as belonging to the tragedy genre.

- The story ends in death.
- Fate works against the protagonist.
- She is pursued and ultimately brought down by the actions of others, although she does have character traits (such as pride and a quick temper) that help to bring about her downfall.

2. Make a list of the ways in which this novel lends itself to adaptation for the screen.

- Hardy's narrator zooms in and out like a camera lens.
- It has moments of danger and action, such as the sleepwalking scene.
- It is structured in distinct parts which would make it easy to adapt for a television series.
- It has a protagonist with whom an audience can sympathise.

3. The narrator in *Tess of the D'Urbervilles* has a patronising attitude towards the protagonist of the novel. Write a paragraph agreeing or disagreeing with this assertion.

- Tess's love for Angel seems naive and idealising to the narrator, who says, 'in her reaction from indignation against the male sex she swerved to excess of honour for Clare' (p. 193).
- The narrator often focuses on physical features, such as her mouth and lips, which make Tess seem like an object on display.
- But the narrator also gives the reader insights into Tess's complex inner self.
- The narrator continues to reinforce Tess's status as a 'pure' woman throughout the novel.

4. Make a list of three moments when the narrator deliberately obscures our perspective or withholds information from us. Briefly note why these shifts in perspective occur.

- We are not told that Tess has succumbed to Alec's temptation at the end of the novel. We must follow her tracks as Angel does. This creates a connection between the reader and Angel, who had previously lost our sympathy through his ill-treatment of Tess.
- We do not hear Tess tell her story to Angel; this happens in the hiatus between Phases four and five. We already know that she was raped and had an illegitimate child, and at this point Hardy is more interested in the effect the narrative has on Angel.

- After the rape scene we are told that an 'immeasurable chasm was to divide our heroine's personality thereafter from that previous self of hers' (p. 74). Hardy leaves a gap of four months after this point to emphasise this transition in Tess's life.

5. Choose three moments when we see the symbolic significance of the colour red, and briefly explain it.

- In the first chapter Tess wears a red ribbon in her hair, which marks her out from her fellow dancers. We could interpret it as a marker of her ultimately tragic fate or as symbolic of her sexuality.
- The piece of blood-stained paper she sees blowing around in Chapter 44 is symbolic of Tess's weariness and the futility of her journey to see Angel's parents in the face of hostile fate.
- Alec is often associated with the red glow of fire (for example, when he seems to almost spring from the fire in Chapter 50). This exacerbates his devilish characteristics.

6. List five words that you find obscure or archaic. Give a dictionary definition for each.

- acclivity (p. 384) – an ascending slope
- effigy (p. 363) – a three-dimensional representation of someone; a statue.
- expostulate (p. 173) – to disagree
- polychrome (p. 122) – multi-coloured
- domiciliary (p. 121) – concerned with the home

7. Compare Angel's speech with Tess's speech when she first arrives at the dairy. Then choose a moment of dialogue between the two characters later on in the novel. What shifts in language use do you find?

- Even before she speaks to Angel, Tess expresses complex ideas, e.g. on p. 120.
- The early dialogues are often structured by Angel questioning Tess.
- After Tess's admission, in Chapter 35, Angel seeks to shut down Tess's attempts at dialogue.
- When they are reconciled in the final chapters of the book, their language is simple and similar.

8. Make a list of three non-visual symbols in the novel. Do they give different effects in contrast to Hardy's visual imagery?

- Music symbolises the connection between Tess and Angel, from her early enchantment with his harp music to her later practising ballads for when he returns from Brazil.
- Tess's voice is identified as 'fluty' and it is the first aspect that attracts Angel's attention.
- The cockerel crow at the end of Chapter 33, just as Angel and Tess set out on their honeymoon, is symbolic of bad luck.

9. Identify three moments in which dialect is used by one of the minor characters. What does it reveal about the character or the context?

- In Chapter 1, Jack Durbeyfield's dialect ' 'Twas said my gr't-grandfer had secrets' (p. 9) provides a stark contrast with Parson Tringham's educated accent.
- In Chapter 4, an unidentified speaker at the village pub says, 'But Joan Durbeyfield must mind that she don't get green malt in flower.' The exact meaning of the local phrase is not revealed here, but it soon becomes clear that it predicts Tess's pregnancy outside of wedlock.
- When Izz tells Angel that 'nobody could love 'ee more than Tess did!' (p. 270), the honesty of her speech is reinforced by her dialect.

10. Identify three significant words or images that recur in the novel, and briefly describe how their meaning alters according to the context.

- Red images recur throughout the text and are most frequently associated with Tess. She wears a red ribbon at the club-walking in Chapter 1. By the end of the novel her once 'rosy' but now whitened hands demonstrate the change she has gone through in becoming Alec's mistress.
- Images of technology and modernity also recur. While the train is representative of the 'ache of modernism' (p. 124) in Tess and connects her to the outside world, the threshing machine emphasises her isolation.
- Images of blood are sometimes found at moments of heightened tension. For example, the narrator focuses on a 'piece of blood-stained paper' (p. 298) when Tess finds the Clares' house empty in Chapter 44. The final culmination of this image is of course the 'gigantic ace of hearts' (p. 382) formed by Alec's spreading blood.

Section Two: Working towards the exam

1. 'In a tragic novel, the protagonist must be flawed in order for their tragedy to be believable.' Do you agree?

- Tess replies 'majestically' (p. 67) to Car Darch's attempts to fight her in Chapter 10. This demonstrates some of the D'Urberville pride that might be argued to contribute to Tess's downfall.
- Tess commits some small acts of violence towards Alec before she murders him. These indicate her quick and passionate temper and suggest the possibility of further violence.
- However, at other moments in the novel Tess seems humble and will not argue against her fate. We see this in her unquestioning acceptance of Angel's decision to leave her.
- A hostile fate seems to have singled Tess out through no fault of her own. Her selfless attempts to help her family bring disaster to herself.

2. How does Hardy uses both time and space to structure his novel?

- Tess's journeys through Wessex mark key moments in the plot and in her character development.
- Tess's family home in Marlott is a key location and its loss brings about the final acceptance of Alec's advances.
- The narrator gestures back to the medieval times of the D'Urberville family's greatness to create a sense of hereditary decline and a linkage between generations.
- Time speeds up or slows down according to the needs of the plot. For example, we spend much time at Talbothays during Tess and Angel's courtship but the period of her life as Alec's mistress is collapsed into a few pages.

3. 'Like many Victorian novelists, Hardy is a realist even when he seems to question the possibilites of realism.' Consider *Tess of the D'Urbervilles* in the light of this statement.

- Like George Eliot, Hardy is interested in subjectivity.
- He also sees an attempt at the truthful representation of the world as part of the novelist's duty.
- He uses free indirect discourse to bring us into the individual's mindset.
- He provides abundant details of setting and environment that enrich the realist narrative.
- Hardy does not glamourise rural life. He demonstrates its difficulties and indignities realistically.

Part Five: Contexts and interpretations

Section One: Check your understanding

1. Make a table demonstrating at least three ways in which wealth and poverty are contrasted in *Tess of the D'Urbervilles*.

- Alec and Angel buy Tess new clothes in attempts to exert control over her.
- Alec's wealth means that he does not have to work, while Tess's (self-enforced) poverty mean that she takes on the hardest tasks of the rural labourer.
- Alec offers Tess's homeless family the building that his mother used to keep her chickens.

2. Make a table contrasting key characteristics of the world of Tess's family with the world of Angel's family.

- Tess's family indulge themselves when they can (e.g. in alcohol); Angel's family are abstemious.
- Tess's family are not particularly interested in religion; their Christian faith determines everything that the Clare family do.
- Tess's family life lurches from crisis to crisis; the Clare family seem to be in greater control of their finances and their destiny.

3. List three forms of technology that play a role in the story of *Tess of the D'Urbervilles*. Include a brief description of the role played by each.

- The train connects rural Wessex to London and the outside world.
- The threshing machine causes a significant shift in the lives of rural labourers.
- The turnip-slicing machine standing opposite the 'grave' (p. 313) in which the roots had been preserved symbolises the cruelty and hardship of the work Tess does at Flintcomb-Ash.

4. Make a list of three reasons why setting is a vital factor in Hardy's work.

- The rural life Hardy depicts was under threat and it was therefore important to try to capture it.
- Tess's life is bordered by the county in which she was born. This contains the action of the story and makes Tess's early naïvety believable.
- Varying the setting allows Hardy to use pathetic fallacy to reflect Tess's changing states in the environment she inhabits.

5. Make a table listing three or four points of connection between *Tess of the D'Urbervilles* and any other text that you have studied.

- *The Mill on the Floss* also has a passionate female protagonist.
- The novel also uses third-person narration to allow us to see the action from a number of perspectives.
- The plot also involves an attempted seduction, but Maggie turns back at the vital moment.

6. Write a paragraph outlining the reasons why Hardy's contemporary critics were shocked when *Tess of the D'Urbervilles* was first published.

- Tess is insistently defined as a 'pure' woman, despite having had an illegitimate child.
- The subject matter, including rape and murder, was seen as inappropriate for a novel by some.
- Some critics did not like Hardy's style and mocked it.

7. Write a paragraph outlining what you understand by the term 'realism'.

- An attempt to represent the world truthfully.
- An emphasis on accurate details in descriptions of setting, dress and dialogue.
- A willingness to represent sordid or unpleasant aspects of life.

8. List three events that might provide focal points for a feminist reading of the novel. Briefly describe the significance of each for such a reading.

- Tess reproaches herself for not helping her mother with the domestic chores (p. 20). This suggests that Tess has taken on the gendered expectation that her life will primarily take place in the domestic rather than the public or professional sphere.
- Alec's rape of Tess and the lack of any legal action or punishment against him demonstrates the sexual double standard that Hardy critiques. It was more acceptable for men than for women to act on their sexual desires.
- Tess's education is cut off before she can attain her ambition of becoming a teacher. A feminist reading would emphasise the inequality of access to education that women have experienced historically.

9. List three moments in the text that a cultural materialist critic might highlight, and explain why.

- The fact that Angel interacts so closely with the family and workers at Talbothays makes cross-class relationships seem integral to the text.
- It is significant that Alec D'Urberville inherits and does not have to work for his money. This makes him lazy and morally suspect in the eyes of Hardy's narrator.
- The lack of possibilities for Tess as a worker and the fact that she ends up earning minimal wages at Flintcomb-Ash confirm the difficulties of rural life.

10. What kind of insights might be gained from an ecocritical reading of *Tess of the D'Urbervilles*? Write a paragraph outlining your ideas.

- A close reading of the scene where Tess and Angel deliver the milk to the train station might focus on the changes to rural life brought by the railway.
- Stonehenge demonstrates how humankind have shaped and altered their natural environment since the earliest civilisations.
- The emphasis on farming, particularly at Talbothays, is suggestive of the possibilities of harmony between humans and their natural world.

Section Two: Working towards the exam

1. Consider the significance of rural life in *Tess of the D'Urbervilles* and in any other novel written in the nineteenth century.

- It allows Hardy to represent a dying culture.
- It allows Hardy to set up a contrast between rural poverty and wealth and to critique the class division.
- In both *Jane Eyre* and *Tess* the protagonists seek isolation and comfort in their rural surroundings during moments of emotional upheaval.

- Rural life is seen from the middle-class perspective of the governess or schoolteacher in *Jane Eyre*, not from the perspective of the rural labourer as in *Tess*.
- The rural setting allows the plots of both novels to be contained and structured by the journeys of the female characters.

2. Examine the relationship between Tess and Angel using three different critical approaches (e.g. feminist, new historicist, Marxist).

- A Marxist reading might emphasise the class difference between the two lovers and suggest that Hardy is providing a critique of his society that often disapproved of cross-class relationships.
- A feminist reading might criticise Angel for his reaction to Tess's revelation of her past sexual experience. His hostility shows that he holds his wife up to a different standard of sexual morality than himself.
- A new historicist reading of the text might read Tess's fate in the light of Darwin's ideas around evolution and extinction and suggest that their relationship was always doomed by the D'Urbervilles' slow movement towards extinction.

3. 'Hardy's novel emphasises how historical forces operate on individual lives.' Do you agree with this statement?

- Yes: Hardy considers the education Tess receives (as part of a movement towards increasing access to education) as important to the formation of her ambitions.
- Yes: Hardy shows how the changes in rural life lead the Durbeyfield family to lose their place in it.
- No: Hardy is more interested in the workings of fate than of history. Sexual desire is the real driving force of the plot and it is not dependent on historical forces.
- No: Hardy demonstrates how Tess's character and decisions as an individual shape her future.

MARK SCHEME

Use this page to assess your answer to the **Practice task** on page 90.

Look at the elements listed for each Assessment Objective. Examiners will be looking to award the highest grades to the students who meet the majority of these criteria. If you can meet two to three elements from each AO, you are working at a good level, with some room for improvement to a higher level.*

> **'All tragic fiction is based on the creation of suspense.'**
>
> **To what extent do you agree with this view in relation to *Tess of the D'Urbervilles*, in terms of how it is constructed by its writer?**

AO1	Articulate informed, personal and creative responses to literary texts, using associated concepts and terminology, and coherent, accurate written expression.	• You make a range of clear, relevant points about how suspense is created, for example by the use of narratorial distancing. • You use a range of literary terms correctly, e.g. **foreshadowing, metaphor**, romance, oxymoron, dialogue. • You address the topic clearly, outlining your thesis and providing a clear conclusion. • You signpost and link your ideas fluently about the creation of suspense within the text. • You offer a personal interpretation which is insightful, well-argued and convincing.
AO2	Analyse ways in which meanings are shaped in literary texts.	• You explain the techniques and methods Hardy uses to create suspense, via the echoing structure through which we expect events to be repeated or amplified later in the text (such as Tess's small acts of violence which create tension and foreshadow the murder) and the use of cliff-hangers as seen between Phases the Fourth and Fifth. • You explain in detail how such examples shape meaning. • You comment on genre, language, setting and structure in a thoughtful, sustained way.
AO3	Demonstrate understanding of the significance and influence of the contexts in which literary texts are written and received.	• You demonstrate your understanding of genre by considering the novel and tragic forms. • Literary context: *Tess* is written at around the same time as Arthur Conan Doyle's *Sherlock Holmes* stories. In these stories the emotional and psychological effects on the victim of crime are not explored as they are in Hardy's text. Conan Doyle creates suspense by having his detective gradually uncover the perpetrator. • Historical or social contexts: the death penalty was used throughout the Victorian period and was still legal in Britain until 1969. Someone committing murder in the nineteenth century would expect to be hanged if brought into custody.
AO4	Explore connections across literary texts.	• You make relevant links between characters and ideas within a text, noting how for example Tess often seems passive or distanced at crucial moments, which creates a sense of suspense as to what might happen to her when she is not in control. • You make critical judgements about the creation of suspense in the text, for example commenting on the melodramatic moments such as Tess's near-death experience with the sleep-walking Angel, and how this creates meaning.
AO5	Explore literary texts informed by different interpretations.	• You reference classical notions of tragedy as defined by Aristotle, Sophocles, etc. and touch on ideas about inevitability, how suspense derives from expectations, and differing ideas about Fate. • You might touch on structuralist readings of the text which focus on the extent to which Tess conforms to cultural ideas of 'tragic fiction' or breaks free of them.

This mark scheme gives you a broad indication of attainment, but check the specific mark scheme for your paper/task to ensure you know what to focus on.